UN-
TYPICAL

UN-TYPICAL

HOW THE WORLD ISN'T BUILT FOR AUTISTIC PEOPLE AND WHAT WE SHOULD ALL DO ABOUT IT

PETE WHARMBY

MUDLARK

Mudlark
HarperCollins*Publishers*
1 London Bridge Street
London SE1 9GF

www.harpercollins.co.uk

HarperCollins*Publishers*
Macken House, 39/40 Mayor Street Upper
Dublin 1, D01 C9W8, Ireland

First published by Mudlark 2023
This edition published 2024

3 5 7 9 10 8 6 4

A catalogue record of this book is
available from the British Library

ISBN 978-0-00-852930-7

Printed and bound in the UK using 100%
renewable electricity at CPI Group (UK) Ltd

For my daughter,
in the hope that this book might help
make the world a better place for her

CONTENTS

INTRODUCTION

If you and I were ever to meet, I doubt you'd suspect a thing. No alarms would be raised or red flags waved as your eyes scanned my face and your ears heard my voice. Reassured, you would talk to me normally. As an equal. As a peer. You would happily assume that I was just like you, and maybe we'd chat for a while: small talk about the weather, sports, you know the kind of topics. Then you would go about your business as you always have, and probably not give me a second thought.

Or ...

If you and I were ever to meet, you'd notice straight away. Your brain – so attuned to tiny variations – would spot all the signs. Those tiny flickers away as I avert my eyes from yours; the slightly slower response times to your questions; the slight – oh, so very slight – traces of panic as our small talk continues. You would be feeling it yourself too, of course. The fatigue of maintaining conversation; the dreaded judgements of what is or isn't a suitable topic for small talk. The awful, wrenching

1

intimacy of even feigned eye contact. You have lived with this all your life. Like me, you can pretend. You can appear 'normal' when necessary. You can mask everything about you that's different and unacceptable, allowing you to maintain some human relationships, and maybe hold down a job. But it's hard. It's so very hard, so exhausting. And here you are talking to another.

Some of you will not understand the previous paragraph. For others, it will be painfully close to the bone, full of things you recognise and dread, things you may have been able to make peace with, or still struggle with to this day.

It all basically depends on whether you're autistic or not.

Interesting fact: we've *absolutely no idea* how many autistic people there are in the world. It used to be set at the suspiciously round number of one in every hundred – a figure still used, even by many major autism charities. There's comfort to be found in that nice, simple '1 per cent' figure, which keeps autistic people very firmly established as a tiny minority. But it's wrong. More recent figures sway wildly from one in sixty to one in twenty-five. That's a huge variation – we obviously don't have a clue what the real number is, but one thing is clear: you share the planet with more autistic people than you ever thought possible.

We're also all at sea about the demographics of the autism community. The accepted idea used to be that the vast majority of autistic people were male. Boys, in fact; it has always been viewed as a childhood condition. As we accelerate into the third decade of the twenty-first century it's becoming clear that this assumption is way out, and that the number of autistic girls and women is probably just as high as the number of autistic boys and men. But news about minorities travels slowly.

What about race? The overriding perception of autism is that it's very white. Black autistic people are still seen as rare and unusual individuals when, in fact, the proportion of Black autistic people is seemingly in line with the proportion in the white community. The same is true for every other ethnicity on the planet. Wherever you find people, you'll find autistics. This has startling implications both historically and in the present, which I will explore later on. To repeat: with a world population of autistic people that could be as big as 230 million, it's likely that you know a lot more of us than you expect, whether we ourselves know it yet or not.

But enough with the numbers. Let's talk stereotypes. Everybody thinks they know what autism is. After all, they've watched *Rain Man*, read *The Curious Incident of the Dog in the Night-Time* and loved Sheldon Cooper in *The Big Bang Theory* (so delightfully *kooky*). They've had their mandatory training on diversity and have combined all this into a vague sense that autistic people are out there and are different, but their understanding is usually pretty crude and ill-formed. Or at least that's the impression I get whenever I talk to non-autistic people either online or in the wild. They exude confidence on the subject, telling me their opinions on neurodiversity (the word, expressing the vast diversity of neurological experience that makes us human, was coined by Dr Judy Singer in the late 1990s) without hesitation – or seemingly any thought at all. 'After all,' they will say, smiling, 'aren't we all somewhere on the spectrum?'

The problem is, autism has gone down the same muddy, over-used path that obsessive–compulsive disorder has found itself wandering down (apparently avoiding the puddles and grouping footsteps into multiples of four, of course). People know the folk myth, not the reality, and it's familiar enough that they deploy it casually when talking about themselves; just one ingredient in the conversational self-diagnostic recipe. A sprinkle of obsession, a dash of compulsion, a soupçon of disorder all add a bit of flavour. 'I just have to have all of my pens lined up nicely and my books in alphabetical order. I'm so OCD!' OCD is the overused coriander of neurology.

And autism is the turmeric – spicier, more noticeable. We're all, if these overconfident folks are to be believed, spiced up with a little pinch of autism; just enough to make us interesting. Neurotypical people recognise just enough autism or 'spectrum-y' in themselves to count themselves 'in the club' and free to let loose with their opinions about it. What autism is. How it works. What it does. How autistic people need to be treated. And these opinions are usually entirely wrong. Not just wrong – actively harmful and even dangerous. As I write this, an American educational centre has been allowed to return to the practice of severely electrocuting their autistic child patients for misdemeanours.* This stems from a complete misunderstanding about how autistic children work, and how to help them. It's also utterly inhumane and disgusting, but then what's new in the treatment of autistic people? This stuff has been going on for years.

This dangerously incomplete and inaccurate understanding of autism, fed annually by well-meaning but ham-fisted attempts to 'raise awareness' by charities run by non-autistic people using language and imagery despised by the autistic community, is everywhere (jigsaw pieces, for example – the idea of autistic people having a 'piece missing' that can be found with sufficient care and attention is increasingly seen as unpleasantly ableist). Because of a lack of proper understanding, people go through life accidentally ignoring, belittling, mocking and hurting actually autistic individuals whose lives and brain architecture can't be summarised in a thirty-second video online or a mediocre character arc in a sitcom. All complexity and nuance are ignored, and the lives of real autistic people are brushed under the huge, thick and slightly musty carpet we call society.

It feels like proper acceptance and understanding of autism are a decade away, at the very least. Until then, we're surrounded by a huge number of problems: a lack of health and social care for autistic children and adults,

---

* Eric Garcia, 'The school that uses shock therapy on autistic students', https://www.independent.co.uk/voices/autism-shock-therapy-trump-biden-b1885595.html, 16 July 2021. Accessed 19 July 2021.

a thousand cobwebbed myths to dust off and send on their way, thousands of well-meaning souls whose understanding of autism is outdated or confused. There's a very long way to go. But you are here. You have picked up this book, so perhaps there's hope. Maybe we can make a start.

I've been autistic all my life. Everybody with autism is the same: we don't 'develop' it, or gain it mysteriously after some routine medical intervention – we're born autistic, live autistic and die autistic. However, and this is the key point, I've not always *known* that I'm autistic. In fact, this pretty crucial information about myself was completely unknown to me until late 2017.

Up to that point I'd been operating under the assumption that I was like everyone else. I'd lived thirty-four years believing I was neurotypical, like everyone else. I grew up learning neurotypical ways. I acted neurotypically, even when it was impossibly difficult. I was like a version of Mowgli from *The Jungle Book*, brought up out of my element, learning how to exist in one world with its terrible dangers while the world I truly belonged to was elsewhere, unknown to me. Unlike him, though, I had no mentor or guide in this journey, no Baloo or Bagheera to help me understand the laws of the jungle. Instead I figured it all out for myself, learning the lingo, maintaining a mask that would not be shifted for decades. I figured out the rules of social interaction gradually, from birth, and with great difficulty. For example:

- Rule 1: You should never ask for something directly – this is an absolute societal red line. If you want something, you must *imply* or *hint* your need for it … somehow.
- Rule 2: If you like someone but don't know them you sort of ignore them; when you're becoming friends you're absolutely lovely to them, then when you're really good friends you treat them very badly.
- Rule 3: To express friendship with an adult male requires a mastery of swearing and insult that would make a nineteenth-century dock worker blush.

All of these were revelations to me, if I'm being completely honest. And while neurotypical people might have flashes of recognition here, I would suggest that these experiences are far less harrowing, confusing and hard to overcome than they are for autistic people. Gradually, I figured out the rules of the neurotypical world. They never made sense to me, but I could play the game well enough to get by (much like how I approach *Cluedo*). Overall, I managed to survive quite well, really. I mean, it was extremely tiring, and I think I knew something, somewhere, was very wrong, but I passed through without anybody speculating that I was different, least of all myself. But suddenly things began to change. A series of huge – and supposedly joyful – life moments (promotion, fatherhood) flung me into a deep depression, with a side portion of anxiety for good measure, and I found myself desperately trying to work out why. Google provided some assistance, in the form of a series of self-administered tests that psychologists use to identify who is or isn't autistic. A score over 32 means you should perhaps begin thinking about approaching a doctor. I scored 70. I emailed my GP that very day.

So now I know what my reality is. I find myself part of a wide autistic community of people who view the world and its peculiarities in much the same way as myself. People who nod knowingly at the dichotomy of being able to give complex lectures on difficult subjects while struggling to tie their shoelaces or remembering to brush their teeth. People who know how exhausting fitting in with the rest of the world can be.

As a fluent speaker of both 'neurodivergent' and 'neurotypical', I'm taking it upon myself here to act as an interlocuter; I'm setting out to translate between these two very different neural demographics, to help the majority understand the minority they have overlooked for so long.

In this book, all of the myths, the half-baked and half-understood factoids, the stale old stereotypes will be set against the real lived experience of an autistic person. The actual experience of being autistic is so much more complicated than these legends, and so much more fascinating. Our brains work in ways that appear to be so alien to the neurotypical population that I'm sometimes left absolutely bewildered by the discrepancy. How can it be, for example, that *implying* something in a weird passive–aggressive way is the default technique when trying to get something done for you? How is it in any way possible that one of the best ways to nurture and feed a friendship is to ask another person 'How are you doing?' incessantly without properly listening to the answer? How is it that isolation – being left with only one's thoughts – is a widespread trope for *unhappiness*, of all things? From my point of view – the point of view of a slightly pissed-off autistic person – all of this is simply beyond reason. And I'm sure that my behaviour appears just as strange to you.

By this point you may have noticed that I'm a little … cross. There's a good reason for this. Since I was diagnosed, I've spoken a great deal on the topic of autism and have written about it even more. I've spoken to, and more importantly listened to, hundreds of autistic people tell me their experiences. My brain acts like a huge sponge most of the time: I can't play a video game without taking in the most esoteric and useless facts, nor can I go on a leisurely walk without my silly eyes taking in every detail of my surroundings, so I can say that I've absorbed *a great deal* of what I've been told. And I'm not happy about it.

The frustration of being punished for a miscommunication, the disappointment of being passed over for job opportunities or turned down for not being 'likeable' enough at interview, the years of terrible confusion and loneliness as they came to terms with their diagnosis. It's the weight of these emotions I absorb. Autistic people are often tremendous empaths, taking on the prevailing emotions in a room and not knowing what to do with them. The sadness, anger, fear, hopelessness. The autistic community I'm a part of is hurting and has been hurting for a long time. So, this is the source of the anger I hold, and it's also a source of the energy that enables me to write this book. Writing a book is not a straightforward thing at the best of times, but for an autistic person it presents a raft of challenges. Without this anger driving me to complete each chapter, each paragraph, each sentence, I doubt I'd have managed it. Fury is an excellent motivator.

What follows is a guide for all of the neurotypicals out there who want to know more about how this secret minority works. I know a lot of people are desperate to do better and make the world a more accessible place. Others will be teetering on the edge of getting themselves booked in for an autism diagnosis (if they can cope with the waiting lists), and I would like this to be useful to them too. Finally, there are the autistic people out there who will enjoy discovering that they're not the only ones who find neurotypicals so completely confusing and comically illogical – this is for you folks too.

I've had thirty-plus years of unhindered access to the neurotypical world and mindset. I was so deeply undercover that I didn't even realise that I *was* undercover, and as a result I can provide both a combination of observations of what autism is really like, and practical steps *you* can take to improve things for your autistic peers, friends, family and children. Things you can do today. Ways you can shift your mindset by just a couple of inches to ensure autistic people fall more firmly within your worldview.

Quick example: wouldn't it be great if society could alter its attitude to the repetitive movements autistic people make when they're stressed? We call these 'stimming', and they help us to self-regulate stress levels. For example, a highly stressed autistic person – let's use me as an example here, as I'm immediately to hand – might rock their hips or twist their feet in order to calm themselves down. I did it myself only a few hours ago while waiting for a phone call, and it works well. The problem is that random unexpected movement is something neurotypicals view with intense suspicion – even alarm.

It's interpreted as anything from drunkenness to a sign of imminent violence – and very much to be avoided. As a result, most autistic people feel an awful lot of shame about this most natural of behaviours (if you're struggling to understand the mechanics of why repetitive movement might soothe us, ask yourself why you pace up and down when you're nervous on the phone …). And feeling shame for this is unreasonable and adds to an autistic person's general feeling of being unwelcome in the world; they cannot be themselves. They must always pretend to be neurotypical, for fear of being shunned by the judgemental majority. But the thing is, people can adjust their expectations. If you see a person wearing sunglasses indoors in a dimly lit space, it might well cross your mind that they could be blind, not just a poseur. As a society we maintain some empathy for blind people.

And imagine! The same could be true for autism. Someone stimming in public – perhaps rocking on a park bench or fiddling with a small toy – could be seen as 'Ah, probably autistic', rather than someone to be feared or avoided. Well, one can dream. Better still – and it's very much what this book is for – we can work to make it happen, in practical and useful ways.

This book represents everything I've learned about autism since I was diagnosed: a summary of my experience as an autistic person making sense of the world as a part of a much larger autistic community. I hope that you find it useful.

DISCLAIMER

I'm only one person and so it's impossible for me to speak for a whole diverse demographic. I'm not speaking for all autistics, nor do I believe that all autistic people are the same. I am, however, a quick learner and a good listener, and I've gathered a lot of information over the years about what it is to be autistic and the commonalities that exist between autistic people, and it's this that forms the backbone of my book. Please don't accuse me of being some bossy voice, speaking over all others – this is hardly the only book on autism to have ever been published. It's my take on things, my experience, my understanding.

1

THE SOCIAL WEB

SMALL TALK RULES

'Hey, Pete, how was your weekend?'

Even though I know it's going to happen, I still grimace with shock every time. Is there any way I can make a break for it and run away without being accused of being too weird? I mean, the stairs are just there, and I reckon I could be down them, out of the door and halfway up the school driveway before the alarm is raised. I'm out of shape, and holding a vast mug of coffee and a stack of exam papers, but given the severity of the situation I think I could still manage it.

But of course, I know the rules well enough to understand that such a move would be labelled 'extreme' and, in all likelihood, 'alarming' by the people I work with, as it's Monday morning at 7.45 a.m. and I've a class to teach in forty-five minutes. Perhaps it's time to acknowledge that escaping into the woods as a response to a typical, innocently asked Monday-morning question is not a viable option. Instead, I will have to respond.

But not honestly, of course. Goodness me, the social *faux pas* were I to respond honestly! No, it's very important, for reasons that I still don't truly understand (I'm thirty-nine), to respond with a vaguely positive remark despite the fact I just had a truly awful weekend; likewise, it's vital not to be *too* positive, as I would then risk appearing a show-off. This morning, so early, so uncaffeinated, I must figure out an appropriate reply and handle any subsequent enquiries. The consequences for getting this wrong have, in the past, been unpleasant; as a result, my anxiety (heart racing, blood pressure building) is depressingly familiar. But it's Monday morning, this person has asked me, and I must try to respond without messing up completely.

I've learned over the course of my life that the correct way to respond to this question is with a simple, meaningless 'Fine, thanks', before continuing with my day. This is 'small talk' – talk without communicative purpose, but brimming with *social* purpose. And it's extremely valuable, at least to the neurotypical majority of people who seem to make all the rules. The purpose of this 'phatic communication', as linguists like to label it, is to lubricate social relationships in tiny increments whenever the situation arises, to give the illusion of meaningful talk while gradually and quietly increasing the connection between the two people.

For an autistic person like myself, it's an absolute nightmare.

There was a time when brand new video games came with a thick instruction booklet that gave you all the information you'd need to get started. I would pore over them before switching the game on, ensuring that I knew exactly what I had to do. It's my understanding that non-autistic people were given – in some subconscious way – something similar to these full, useful pamphlets filled with rules and guidance and tips and tricks for the game called *Social Interaction* the moment they were born. Meanwhile, my autistic peers and I received nothing, leaving us to try to piece together the 'rules' without any kind of assistance, forever feeling slightly locked out of the full experience of 'life'.

It's true that autistic people often report feeling like they grew up without access to whatever social rule book it is that non-autistic folk appear to have automatic access to, and it will be a metaphor that I will bring up regularly, by necessity. As we watch our neurotypical peers, we realise that all of this stuff comes naturally, *automatically*, to them, while we autistic people seem to be stuck on manual, struggling to keep up. Small talk seems as easy for them as clapping, but for the autistic population it's a barrier that thwarts us several times a day. Why is this?

Autistic people of an age where small talk has long become commonplace – usually in employment – will have experienced years of both misunderstanding other people and being misunderstood in turn. It's a common feature of autism and can be quite disabling. Being understood can be compared to an aeroplane's autopilot. For many non-autistic people, conversations are relatively easy. Thanks to the instinctive understanding of the rule book, they go smoothly and serenely from point to point, like an airliner calmly progressing to its destination, safe in the hands of automation. Exactly the same interaction for most autistic people is more akin to piloting an aircraft with no autopilot, and very little training, through a major city (one filled with skyscrapers) in the fog. Every movement of the controls veers you wildly in varying, unpredictable directions and you feel – and I can't stress this strongly enough – as if you're always moments from disaster.

The accepted rules of conversation were a mystery to me, at least at first, and progress towards gradually acquiring them was slow and frustrating. There's a lot of unspoken content in a typical conversation, and I'm not only referring to body language and facial expression. An awful lot of communication is entirely implicit, needing to be inferred accurately in order to understand whatever point the other person is making, and it's this content that can cause autistic people the biggest problems. I think it's fair to claim, although I say this as someone with a degree in English Literature so I may be biased, that autistic people are OK with implied meaning *in theory*, and understand the concept; it's the speed and complexity of natural speech that causes problems as we tend to need more time to process whether implication is actually taking place, whereas non-autistic people seem to know straight away.

For example, someone I care about could drop into our conversation the fact that they're cold. I might be aware that the window's open, there's six inches of snow on the ground outside and they're wearing a T-shirt, but it's extremely unlikely that I'd spot the implication and close the window or offer them a sweater. It simply would not occur to me that their statement was anything more than a simple statement of fact. After all, if they truly wanted me to do something, wouldn't they ask, rather than just hint in such a vague way? The whole thing is so fraught with uncertainty: even if I *had* spotted the implication, it's likely I'd then spend a frantic few moments second-guessing myself in a panic – 'But what if they *don't* mean that and I end up looking presumptuous?' – by which time they've probably given up and closed the window themselves. A large portion of human interaction, at least in the English-speaking world, relies on this infuriatingly meandering and tricky method of communicating information.

Small talk is a version of this, in my opinion. The vague introductory remarks and questions ('Warm today, isn't it?', 'Monday mornings, eh?') are not direct and they're emphatically not looking for factual, literal responses. Instead, I must understand that what's *really* required here is a response that's similarly vague (almost meaningless, in fact) and that I'm then meant to move away from the conversation. As I, and the majority of autistic people generally, tend to miss this implication, you can see where the problem lies. Upon hearing 'Warm today, isn't it?' my natural reaction is to reply with either yes or no, depending on the ambient temperature. This isn't some infuriating quirk that autistic people have because we're weird – we're actually using language as it appears to have been intended. But if I *were* to reply truthfully with a 'No, I think it's quite cold actually,' I'd immediately be viewed as strange, combative and contrary. All for answering a damned question accurately.

It wouldn't be so bad if this were an example of a 'white lie', where responding with honesty causes understandable misery or disappointment for the other party. I mean, how much does this person care about how warm it is? By their likely reaction to my disagreeing with them, you'd think the temperature of the room was something they'd worked hard to achieve, were very proud of and would fight to preserve, like how a new dress looks. But obviously this is rarely the case and the discomfort is caused not by actual grievance or even emotion – it's caused entirely by going against what's *customary*.

It's endlessly fascinating to me how important *custom* is to the majority of people. As an autistic person I can certainly see the value of the familiar and the routine, but I struggle to understand the need for these scripted, stock responses. I understand that small talk is more about the 'social' in 'social communication' than the 'communication', that content is less important than simply connecting and that there's even a fear of silence at play too; but despite all this, the likely negative reaction were I to break script seems disproportionate. The fact that small talk, this means of quickly bolstering relationships and politeness, is so prone to wreck an autistic person's day seems like a serious flaw in the entire system, but most autistic people would recognise this unfairness with a shrug, as it's so commonplace.

* * *

If we swing back to the Monday-morning scenario we started with when my colleague asks me how my weekend was while I stand at the photocopier, the expectation is clear. My colleague, with all the goodwill in the world, expects me to respond with something approximating 'Fine, thanks'. If I do this, the interaction will cease, with him being satisfied by its perceived success while I'm left dissatisfied by the lack of honesty and sincerity I was forced into. Thinking about all the times this kind of interaction has left me feeling stressed and unhappy, it's the dishonesty that hurts the most. By responding with a 'Fine, thanks', I will have lied twice. Once with the 'fine' – my weekend was awful and I'm still feeling terrible about it (hence the huge coffee) – and second with the 'thanks' – I've nothing to be thankful for here: they've just forced me to lie about my feelings when I would rather have said nothing at all.

By this point I'd sympathise with you if you're starting to think I'm overthinking the whole thing. But that's the problem – overthinking is what autistic people do, to the point I'm surprised it isn't among the diagnostic criteria. If you take a moment to glance back over the pages of this chapter so far and get a feel for the number of words I've dedicated to this single interaction, you'd come close to having a visual metaphor of how active and turbulent the inside of my head is during a tiny moment like this.

If only these moments were rare. Instead, they're very frequent, and if, as I did for fifteen years, you work in a location with lots of other staff, it can be expected that such dissatisfying, stressful interactions will occur *multiple times a day*. It stands to reason that any autistic person struggling with small talk will eventually hit some kind of wall, causing us to mess up completely. It's the times this has happened that keep me awake at night – where rather than swallowing my discomfort and answering according to the script, I instead forgot and went dangerously off-piste or, worse still, actually did run away to the woods to begin a new life as some kind of extremely tall squirrel. The more stressed I am (and as you will come to learn, stress is a huge part of my life), the more likely I am to forget what the rules are and make a fool of myself. One example sticks out in my mind, though – not because it was particularly embarrassing, but because of how unexpectedly *well* the neurotypical person in the exchange responded to my 'failure' to follow the rules.

It was the day before the Christmas holidays, the last day of term, and I was heading out of the building with a bag full of students' work to mark. The headteacher was standing by the door, so small talk was unavoidable, and I was really not feeling very well. He chatted briefly about this and that, before mentioning how he was worried about the kids who were going back to stressful home lives, who had school as a way of keeping them safe and calm. I was having a very rough time at home with a new baby and lack of sleep, and blurted out without thinking: 'That's how I feel. It's like work is this safer space where I can find some calm even though teaching really stresses me out, whereas home is this exhausting, relentless nightmare.'

Amazingly, I had managed to both overshare *and* confess that the core part of my job was causing me serious problems. And all at Christmas time, to a headteacher whom I can't say I was particularly close to or friendly with at this point. To his credit, my boss took this sudden declaration of misery on the chin and empathised by muttering a word or two on how hard it all sounded, before I ran to my car to have a brief but memorable panic attack at the steering wheel before turning the ignition. This exchange hounded me for the entirety of the Christmas holiday that year, only briefly fading in the evenings when I'd had a few glasses of beer, as I couldn't stop myself dissecting the moment and trying to second-guess how he was likely to respond in the new year. It's a process I'm very familiar with, whereby I consider every possible likely outcome that I can imagine, and try to figure out how I'll cope with it should it come to pass, rather like when Doctor Strange visits millions of future timelines searching for the one where the Avengers win the day.

It's important at this juncture to recognise that this level of obsessive over-analysis of a 'failed' communication is by no means unusual or a one-off. It's the standard, or at least it is for me and vast numbers of autistic people who can share similar tales. In fact, in this example I at least has some good reason to be worried, given the nature of the employee–employer relationship. The sad thing is, I've undergone the same kind of extreme 'over-thinking' about small talk that went only blandly and meaninglessly wrong, like the time I told a distant colleague whose name I didn't even know that I'd had a terrible bout of food poisoning over the holiday and indulged in some choice details. Why?

Well, she asked me, upon bumping into me on the street, how my holidays had been. She walked away shaken. As did I.

This was never going to lead to anything tangibly *bad* happening, and I knew that well enough at the time. It was embarrassing, yes; it even approached being funny, in certain lights, but it would never cause any significant problems. Despite this, I was absolutely obsessed with my 'failure' for weeks, possibly months (and this was back in 2008 or so, years before my diagnosis), as I was convinced that it would somehow transform into something awful. Of course it never did. I still worry about it from time to time.

As for the headteacher, spring term began and there were no repercussions following my brief moment of oversharing. Things in that job did begin to deteriorate, mostly as a result of being diagnosed as autistic, but I don't believe that the exchange played much of a part in this. The one thing I did notice, however, was that my boss became an awful lot more approachable after this and was a source of great support for several years. I like to think that he responded to my autistic inability to judge the nature of small talk in the best way – by accepting it at face value and taking it on board, rather than judging me for daring to go off-script. If more people were capable of this, perhaps autistic people would begin to feel more comfortable.

DIFFICULT CONVERSATIONS

Everyone seems to love talking. They all seem to do it so much, so freely, so oblivious to the risks it contains. It must be fantastic to be able to converse with so little care or worry, to go through life seeing conversation as just another minor pleasure. Sadly, talking with other people – in particular non-autistic people – has so many pitfalls and dangers for most autistic people, that they're scarred by a form of chronic, constant trauma that's hard for non-autistic people to imagine. The problem lies, as it so often does, in those ironically 'unwritten' rules that everybody has to abide by. Rather like the unwritten constitution of the United Kingdom, this leads to extreme ambiguity and reliance on precedent, neither of which are particularly well suited to the average autistic person. We tend to slide from crisis to crisis when talking to people, and behind it all is a brain whirring over the potential problems, analysing every facet.

It's so unclear how so much of it works. Turn-taking is a good example. All conversations are built on the idea of the back-and-forth, and it seems to be implicitly understood by most people when these moments of shift should occur. But not to me. I've *no idea* when it's OK for me to take my turn, and so I often find myself sitting very quietly, intently waiting for a pause long enough to represent an unambiguous jumping-off point. By the time I feel the coast is clear for me to interject my opinions on a subject, the conversation has rumbled off into the distance and I'm left nursing an unshared idea.

Some people seem to be allowed to interrupt at will, powerfully diverting a chat in their preferred direction without anyone being noticeably bothered by their rudeness. The few times I tried this tack I was invariably met by a sea of ruffled, cross faces, aghast at my arrogance. Confused, I'd back down and quietly apologise, wondering what magical aura surrounded those who have everyone's permission to interrupt. The fact is, there's no discernible logic to turn-taking in neurotypical conversation. It just happens, and it happens fairly well, with interactions only occasionally going wrong. If I'm around, that likelihood ratchets up by several dozen percentage points. These rules are not built into my autistic brain. For whatever reason, the set of rules I follow are desperately incompatible with the ones you follow. It's like we're speaking different languages.

A very common trait that many autistic people share is a desire to share information about our special interests. I will go into more detail later in the book about how these interests work and the benefits they bring; for now, it's important to know that all that knowledge and passion we have for the topic *needs sharing*! Like all the best altruists, we're so often desperate to talk about this stuff because we want you to be as well informed and fascinated as we are. A lot of autistic adults will have learned the hard way that this desire to share is not met in the same spirit, and as such will force themselves to not mention it. The problem is that the earnest zeal with which we approach our favourite things is very rarely matched by the neurotypical listener. I've often pondered whether neurotypical people are even capable of the same intense level of interest in a topic.

The trouble is, we tend to get rather carried away, and I believe that it's fair to say that we often forget that our level of love for, say, *Super Mario* or knitting is not shared by those we're talking to. As a result, our passionate explanations about why *Super Mario Bros. 3* is *still* the best instalment in the series, in lots of detail, possibly with diagrams, tend to be met by alarm and fear, or at the very least utter boredom. We may struggle to identify others' emotions (and our own, truth be told), but I wager most autistic people will eventually notice the boredom on the face of the person we're sharing with – usually because it's paired with them telling us to shut the hell up. This hurts. We love our interests and much of the time see them as one of the only topics *worth* discussing – I mean, surely it's better than small talk? – and talking about them is so intensely joyful, as well as being cathartic and stress-relieving.

It always feels to me that the neurotypical world puts arbitrary limits on how passionate one is 'allowed' to be about a subject. Crossing this line is a social *faux pas* that ranks somewhere around telling inappropriate jokes at a funeral, but it isn't based on anything real or important. More likely, it's some kind of filter that separates people out based on their earnestness – in the UK at least it can feel as if such earnestness is a flaw, unacceptable to the majority. The anthropologist Kate Fox made this argument very convincingly in her book *Watching the English*, and I wonder whether the autistic desire to share deep knowledge is better received in other, less performatively indifferent countries. It's ironic, though, that many of those same people who are put off by autistic levels of interest in a topic will happily watch football pundits discuss the intricacies of a match for ages, or spend hours upon hours memorising the lyrics to every single Taylor Swift song, as well as the singer's entire biography.

It seems to this autistic person that the real problems in communication tend to occur when the line between neurotypical and neurodivergent is crossed in whatever way. There seems to be a reasonably consistent consensus among autistic people that conversing with fellow autistics is much easier, less prone to breakdown or collapse, with a shared understanding of our version of the 'rules' (or at least a much greater tolerance of different ways to do the talking). Autistic people seem to have a much greater capacity to hear about other autistic people's special interests too – a useful trait, given how special interests are so important to us. In contrast, trying to cross over the neuro-barrier is very difficult and likely to lead to dissatisfaction on both sides. This is so frequently painted as a problem that lies squarely at the feet of the autistic person, that it has been absorbed as a kind of internalised ableism. It's too easy to think, in a defeatist, miserable way, that we're the ones who keep messing up and that we're the ones, therefore, who need to change (somehow; I'm not convinced that change of this type is possible, and if it is then it certainly isn't sustainable).

The reality is that navigating the confusing thickets of conversation is a two-way street – it takes two to tangle, as it were – and so neurotypicals have just as much of an imperative to compromise as we do. Autistic academic Dr Damian Milton has written at length, and very persuasively, of the 'double-empathy problem' (it's well worth reading up on), which explores the fact that though autistic people may struggle to understand neurotypical viewpoints, neurotypicals have just as much difficulty understanding us. The difference is that we're hyper-aware of our struggle and go out of our way to compensate for the difference, while you lot (with the greatest respect) don't seem to have a bloody clue.

Meeting part-way seems to be the best outcome here, where the efforts autistic people make to try to under-stand your odd rules and preferences are matched by an effort on your part to do the equivalent; perhaps then we might find ourselves, if not conversing with slick ease, then at least not getting *too* upset by our mistakes and flubs. Give us space to talk, and ask us if we wish to participate, forgive us if we inadvertently interrupt, and be kind if we mistake your grimace of boredom for full-on enthusiasm when we get started talking about the history of the Jedi and their various fighting styles.

WEARING THE MASK

There's something about eye contact in Western society that's peculiar, at least to my autistic eyes. It seems to be held in such high regard for something so fleeting and ambiguous, and the general rule of thumb appears to be that eye contact equals trustworthiness. Far be it from me to question such a bizarre belief (as if liars are incapable of eye contact, and that's their singular weakness …); it's enough to note that there are many good reasons why eye contact may be impossible at any given moment, and that placing such high value upon it might therefore be rather ill-advised. But I'm powerless in the face of our social attitudes. The fact is, for good or ill, that eye contact seems to be very important to lots of neurotypical types and you often base huge decisions upon it. This is a real problem for us autistic people.

You see, for us there's something about eye contact that makes it sensitive to the point of serious intimacy. Making eye contact beyond very fleeting micro-moments of direct pupil-to-pupil alignment is something we'd rather do only with those whom we're comfortable to fart in the presence of. It's a behaviour limited to our closest, most precious relationships: partners, husbands, wives, children. Even my closest friends would probably say I tend to avoid it.

Why this is the case is hard to explain – after all, there's no centrally issued pamphlet explaining every aspect of autism. We autistic folks have had to figure it out for ourselves, and I'm just one of many mouthpieces trying to explain all of this to the rest of the world. However, there are some possible explanations, the most obvious being that it's simply another manifestation of how our neurology differs considerably from everyone else's. It may be that it's similar to our lack of interest in small talk, and our favouring of clear, unambiguous language: a communicative difference where (for us) eye contact has a very different *meaning* when viewed as some kind of body language. Rather than meaning something along the lines of 'I trust you and am listening to you,' as it seems to for our neurotypical brethren, perhaps it's more a statement of 'I trust and like you so deeply that you're probably the only person I'll look into the pupils of for the rest of the decade.'

On the other hand, it may be linked with our sensory sensitivity. For the great majority of autistic people, our senses seem to be calibrated in peculiar ways. Sometimes it can feel that every touch, or light, or sound, or smell is way too intense and horrifying, while at other times it's the exact opposite, and everything can feel deadened and strangely numb and quiet. We talk more about the 'hypersensitivity', though, because it tends to have the bigger and more detrimental impact on our lives. Imagine if every time someone touched you it hurt, or if every light appeared dazzling and harsh, or if every sound came as a terrifying loud shock: that's how being autistic can feel, much of the time. When stress levels are higher, the sensitivity seems to get even worse – or at least that's how it works for me. Many autistic people report unwanted eye contact to be painful in this way – almost like staring at the sun but without the warmth. For anyone forced to make prolonged eye contact (for example, children in some school environments), it can become so uncomfortable as to cause a meltdown. This fits in with the general feeling of sensory overload and would explain why we avoid it so assiduously.

Either way, it's clearly not the kind of thing we ought to be forcing ourselves to do, and yet here we are, living in a system where we must do exactly that on a daily basis in order to appease those around us, who rarely know what it is they're asking us to do. Autistic people are regularly labelled as rude, evasive or untrustworthy based on this one trait alone, and we very quickly learn that if we want to have a relatively pain-free experience dealing with neurotypicals, we're going to have to make eye contact some of the time. This energy-draining, majority-pleasing, difficult act is what we call 'camouflaging' or, more often, 'masking'.

Masking is something that almost all autistic people will learn to do at some point in their life. It often begins in childhood when we realise that something is apparently 'wrong' with us. We notice that our social skills don't seem to cut it, that we're frequently at a loss to understand what's going on, and that our attempts to make and keep friends are clumsier or less successful than our peers. We learn that the depth of our interests and the way we express that passion is unacceptable to everyone else, and that our sensory sensitivity annoys people who don't seem to ever want to understand it. Frequently, we're mistreated because of all or some of these things; sometimes we're bullied; occasionally even abused. In this apparently life-or-death situation, it becomes clear to us that we're going to have to adapt, and so, usually by ourselves and with very little assistance from anyone else, we learn to mask.

We learn to adopt a kind of persona – based on all the things our extremely observant brains have noticed in other people – in order to please those around us so they stop bullying us or causing us harm. As some autistic advocates and researchers (such as Dr Amy Pearson and

Kieran Rose) have been trying to make clear, this is first and foremost a trauma response, the result of trying to avoid the consequences that frequently stem from being autistic in a non-autistic world. It's a kind of fawning to the aggressor, subliminally saying, 'I will be whoever you need me to be, just don't hurt me.' It's often extraordinarily successful – considering it's usually self-taught – and is one of the main reasons why so many autistic people slip through the diagnostic net and only realise they're neurodivergent much later in life: we're so unwittingly good at 'fooling' others that we manage to 'fool' ourselves too.

This is how it was for me. Looking back to my childhood, I think I must have begun masking (all unconsciously – this was not a specific decision I made) around the age of five or so. This was when I first went to school and had to deal with a more concentrated dose of 'other children', who must have taken umbrage at my autistic self. My personal form of masking very quickly developed. I always sought to be as inoffensive and unnoticeable as possible, which, I suppose my young brain reasoned, was the easiest way to avoid being attacked for my obvious foibles. And so I sank into the background, the very definition of a wallflower, and avoided ever making a fuss or, worse, a 'scene'. I often wonder if any of my teachers either noticed me or would remember me; I doubt it very much.

As such, my childhood passed. Autistic people frequently report using elements of personalities they observe – a friend, perhaps, or even a favourite fictional character – as building blocks for their mask, almost as if we're constructing them out of LEGO bricks, and I can certainly empathise with this. I would study (still do, though at least now I'm more aware of what I'm doing) personalities with the care of a collector, trying things on like a shopper in the market for a new pair of jeans. Over time my mask, so separate from myself, began to be as complex as my own personality. I'm loath to suggest that this constructed mask was a total deception or lie, as it wasn't deliberate or designed to confound. But it was a layer of pretence. It was acting, but without a script. Interestingly, neurotypical people can mask too – we call it 'confidence', and it's pretty common to see an introvert 'put on a brave face' at a party, for example. However, for these people masking is more of a choice – it's not a matter of life-and-death as it can so often feel for autistic people. The act is there not to make us fit in at a party, but to make us fit in with *humanity* – the act has much higher stakes.

This is why masking is so tiring. People can't be expected to put on an act all day. Even Daniel Day-Lewis would struggle to maintain a role for years, after all; I'm certain that he'd be desperate to retire to his trailer to relax after only a long afternoon. Donning that mask when socialising or – worse, harder still – at work is an energy-sapper of overwhelming proportions. Imagine attaching an electric heater to your smartphone, feeding from the same battery, and imagine how often you would end up panicking about only having 10 per cent left on your battery as a result, while on the bus miles from home. This gets you a little closer to how it feels to be masking all the time, only *you* are the phone that's about to die. People joke about the joy of removing shoes or a bra after a long day at work – well, the same can be said of autistic masks. Walk through the door, fling it onto the back of the sofa, and let your real self sink and rest into its more natural position.

When I was diagnosed as autistic I still worked as a teacher – I had done for ten years – and I realised pretty quickly that my teaching style, from my facial expressions to my voice, was another form of sophisticated masking: a mask atop another mask, if you like. The mask I'd learned to wear since childhood was the one I donned to handle the ordinary social aspect of teaching, such as chatting with colleagues or taking part in meetings. The mask I wore when a class of thirty fourteen-year-olds filled my classroom was different, even more of a performance, even more extroverted and, as a result, an awful lot more tiring. As soon as I was alone after a lesson I'd find myself collapsing into my chair, feeling utterly drained and forlorn. Typically I'd have to sit and rest – not in a 'chat with buddies in the staff-room' way; more 'sit not moving with my eyes closed', trying to prevent a migraine from setting in from the exertion.

There's a large number of autistic teachers in the world and my respect for them is huge – managing to keep up this cycle of masking/recovery is unsustainable and causes terrible problems, and yet so many continue to push on, day by day. If it had not been for the Covid pandemic, I'm certain that I'd still be in the classroom – completely broken, but too scared to walk away. Happily (and I use the adverb without irony), one positive thing that the horror show of the first few years of the 2020s did for me was force my hand. I'm glad it did.

To take stock: masking is a very tiring thing, and we autistic people feel, for the most part, that we're forced into it by a society who cannot accept us for who we are. It's impossible to sustain forever, however, so there has to come a point where we drop the mask. And what inevitably happens when we do this? The answer is as predictable as it is depressing: we're immediately reminded why we put it on in the first place. An interesting phenomenon that many late-diagnosed autistic people report is that straight after their diagnosis, their relationships with their family, friends and especially work colleagues start to break down a little. This is frequently inexplicable and without clear cause, but the truth of the matter makes for a grim realisation.

Often – and I did this myself, without being aware of it – we instinctively relax a little on finding out we're autistic. There's a strange catharsis in finding out you're neurodivergent, a kind of epiphany that there's a reason *why* things are the way they are. As a result, we exhale for the first time in years, lean into our autistic traits a little, let our mask slip and … well, we pay the price almost immediately. We learn *very* quickly that our unmasked selves are simply not welcome and so we hurriedly fix our masks back on – nail them firm for fear of them dislodging – and realise we'll never be free to be ourselves.

I think of all the concepts elaborated in this book, masking is the one that has caused autistic people the most problems. This is so deeply ironic than I can scarcely stop myself giving a bitter, hollow laugh at the absurdity of it all, but I believe it to be the case. The problem is that successful masking can delay diagnosis – and, even more insidiously, also delay the preliminary *self-diagnosis* many of us had to make before seeing a doctor – for years and years, usually until some kind of crisis moment occurs that forces ourselves, and our doctors, to seek out what is really going on. Masking's subconscious nature means it can hide our true neurotype even from ourselves, stopping us from understanding who we really are.

And even after diagnosis, when we know what's going on in our own heads, masking to get through the day can wildly misrepresent our needs: who's going to help us when we're so adept at appearing to glide painlessly through life? It's a Catch-22. We mask because we have to, but in doing so we cause ourselves so much harm that we're never able to unmask. Round and round it goes.

If you're going to make life easier for the autistic people around you, then gradually allowing us to drop our mask is crucial. However, this comes with a huge proviso: you need to be able to handle whoever lies behind it. You must manage to adapt your expectations of your friend or family member, and show them that their true selves are even more welcome than their masked personas. It's upsetting how rarely this happens and how often we must retreat back behind the mask, ashamed of ourselves for being so unacceptable even to our own *friends*.

MELTDOWNS

There's a reason beyond simple compassion and empathy for why it's so important that an autistic person's needs are met: the result, should we be pushed for too long and too hard. Like any other human being, an autistic person has a threshold – a ceiling of just how much crap they can take before something has to give. I have to emphasise here that there's nothing unusual about this whatsoever – every single person reading this will have had some kind of emotional outburst when things just got too much to handle. It's vital that we understand this universal of human experience because it helps to put autistic meltdown into perspective.

For many non-autistic people, autistic meltdown is one of the more notorious aspects of autism. There are many reasons for this, I suppose: first, meltdowns can be quite noticeable, so if you happen to be out shopping and an autistic person is having one (and who can blame them if it's a particularly busy Saturday), then it's likely you'll notice it. Second, they're a real favourite of non-autistic writers who seek to insert autistic characters into their books and shows. I guess the drama of a meltdown is an attractive feature. It's therefore likely that any fictional representation of autism will include – probably very prominently – an autistic meltdown of some kind. Third, meltdowns are an aspect of autism that's fixated upon by non-autistic parents and carers, who often try to gain some sympathy by putting videos on YouTube of their autistic kids having severe meltdowns. Combined, there's a powerful narrative, constructed mostly by non-autistics, that witnessing autistic meltdown is an absolute nightmare and a constant source of stress and horror.

This may well be the case, my non-autistic friends. But you try actually experiencing one first hand.

I've had many meltdowns in my life. Some in public, all of which I remember with an overwhelming yet unreasonable sense of shame, and many in private. For many years I'd no idea what they were, nor what caused them – I assumed they were simply tantrums, and that I had a bad temper or was particularly childish (it's amazing how cruel a person can be to themselves when trying to explain behaviour caused by a disability they don't know they have). And this is also how meltdowns can be couched by non-autistic people. There are hundreds if not thousands of autistic people who've been accused of throwing tantrums by professionals – doctors and teachers – when what's actually happening is *something else entirely*.

Generally speaking, when a neurotypical person hits a ceiling of tolerance and an explosion of emotion occurs, they then receive an awful lot of love and support from the people around them. They recognise that the person has been pushed to their limits because they themselves have similar limits. They know that they wouldn't be able to take that level of abuse or trauma without snapping, and so they can pour affection and support onto the affected person. We see this frequently when people have experienced serious stress, from divorces to deaths to moving house to being robbed. There are mountains of compassion for these individuals. However, when an autistic person goes through precisely the same process, they often receive none. Why the double standard?

The reason is because the non-autistic onlookers do not recognise the different limits. They see an autistic person melting down in, say, a restaurant, and reason that their surroundings and situations do not warrant such a reaction. They know that *they themselves* can handle being in a noisy restaurant, so why on earth is that person over there freaking out? The understanding that's lacking is that autistic people are already, just by being alive in this world, close to their natural limit of stress – their ceiling of tolerance. We exist just beneath that line, all of the time, whereas non-autistics, for the most part, spend their lives way beneath it, barely even aware that there's a line, until something dreadful happens and you suddenly find yourself crossing it. Our lives *are* the line, and thus we cross it frequently. This, I believe, is why there's so rarely any compassion or care shown to autistic people in meltdown: we're not seen to *deserve* such a reaction as the situation doesn't appear to *warrant* it.

You can feel a meltdown coming. Autistic people often say that we try to get ourselves into a safe, quiet area so we can either decompress at our own speed or have the meltdown in private without interruption and shame afterwards. For there is shame. I'm old enough, and got diagnosed late enough, to have internalised whole heaps of ableism, and I therefore struggle to see my meltdowns as anything other than big adult tantrums. This is how they've been presented to me throughout my life, and how I've been treated, and it's very difficult to unlearn all of that. I would never view anyone else's meltdown as a tantrum, you understand; no, that cruel assessment is reserved only for myself. Shame is a very likely after-effect of a big meltdown: shame that you were seen in such a state, shame at the things you may have said, or done, in the heat of the moment.

Once the meltdown is incoming, it can be headed off: if I'm allowed to calm myself, and have been removed from whatever stimulus has triggered it, I've been able to avoid falling into full-blown meltdown with reasonable success. But assuming it isn't avoided, it will begin. Now, I cannot speak for all autistic people on *any* topic, but I feel that most strongly here: all autistic people will have a meltdown in different ways, so I will only describe how it feels for myself.

It feels terrifying.

The worst thing is the loss of control. It always seems as if there's some tiny portion of my brain that's still working, but it's pushed harshly into a corner and can do little more than chirrup uselessly while the remainder of my brain explodes like fireworks in unison. I lose the ability to properly communicate. Unlike many autistic people, I can still talk during meltdown to an extent, but my words are muddled and their tone will invariably be more aggressive than I would normally intend. My muscles seem to clench as one in some bizarre rictus, making it difficult to move and even harder to be comfortable. My brain is best described as being static, like we used to see on old analogue televisions when they weren't tuned in. It's painful. Focus is impossible. Every part of my body seems to be furiously weighing up the options of 'fight or flight' and finds the best result will surely be attempting both simultaneously.

I'll invariably find myself on the floor, possibly curled up, maybe crying, though not necessarily. I may well be making repetitive movements – stimming – but in a much more intense yet poignantly futile way than normal. Perhaps it helps, but it certainly doesn't feel like it's very effective. My body does it anyway. In the worst examples I've been known to punch my own legs, scratch my own arms until they're red raw or even bang my head against things. I write this now dispassionately, an observer aware of how peculiar it may sound that someone who's very comfortable delivering speeches to large audiences, writing books and teaching students could end up suffering in this way. It's pretty hard to imagine, if you were to meet me, that this kind of thing happens. But it does, and that's autism: a hidden disability.

If I'm lucky, all of this will be over within perhaps half an hour. But the hangover will last much longer. Usually, I'll be feeling the after-effects of meltdown for a day or two – often these are days that can be pretty much written off, as nothing productive can be achieved in such a state. Overall, the average meltdown will ruin a whole day, damage a further two days, damage my relationships with those present (and myself), and leave me physically exhausted, if not actively hurt.

There's a second type of meltdown that seems to be just as prevalent as the first, and this we call 'shutdown'. It's a much more passive and less aggressive form of break, where the autistic person reaches something approaching a state of catatonia for a short period in response to continued exposure to intolerable stress. It can involve a total loss of all communication, as well as an inability to move or even to think. It's less intense than a meltdown, less intrusive, but actually quite scary in itself. I've experienced fewer of these in my lifetime and I'd rather never have to deal with one again.

This is all rather heavy. I understand that. I also understand that many reading this will have experienced meltdowns or shutdowns from an external perspective and know how frightening they are. People often ask me and other autistic adults, 'What can we do to avoid meltdown in others?' and my answer is always the same: respect the autistic person's autonomy. Most of us know what we need to do when meltdown is pelting down the tracks at us – we need to extricate ourselves from the source of stress, immediately, and go somewhere with as little stimuli as possible – a quiet room of some kind, where our stress levels can gradually drop and we can recover. It's quite simple, but it's astonishing how rarely this occurs. Too often, non-autistic people are too busy criticising or even punishing the autistic person for whatever perceived terrible behaviour they showed in the early stages of meltdown (for example, leaving the room – an incredibly common one that's also infuriating because although it's apparently 'rude', it's also an automatic failsafe to avoid escalation).

Too often autistic people are followed from room to room as they try to escape the stressor that's assailing them, they're shouted at and challenged. In these circumstances meltdown is completely unavoidable, and is even actively encouraged by those failing to 'read the room'. Autistic people must be allowed to self-isolate in order to recuperate. When it comes to autistic children in meltdown, this may not work so well – after all, you cannot simply wander off and let a four-year-old regain composure alone in the middle of a motorway service station.

For children, it can be a good idea not to get too hands-on (unless you know that's a good method for them), so don't try to smother them in cuddles; this might be too much and can even exacerbate the meltdown. Instead, give them a metre or so space, don't tell them off and remind them in gentle tones that it's OK, and that you're going to stick around and wait with them while they become calm. It's a good idea to have a series of calming activities established in advance – a kind of emergency kit – that can be called upon. Anything from encouraging them to breathe deeply, to 'blowing out their fingers' (a wonderful practice my daughter learned at nursery school, where they blow on their outstretched fingers like birthday candles, one at a time, until they become more relaxed), to doing a little colouring or singing can work. Then it may simply be a case of reminding them to 'breathe' or 'sing'.

Of course, it's also possible to reduce the stressors in the first place – identify those things that cause a huge uptick in stress levels and, where possible, remove a need for them or try to find ways of avoiding them. All of the advice about social communication I gave earlier in this chapter can be seen as an example of this, as can – to pluck a random example from the air – not forcing autistic people to do things they frequently literally cannot stand, like making phone calls ...

PHONE PHOBIA

I've always assumed that autistic people were generally happier before the 1870s. Life must have been a balmy, relaxed dream, spending all day safe in the certain knowledge that you were never going to be expected to answer a ringing telephone. Then Alexander Graham Bell sauntered along and shattered this peaceful world with his squalling, intrusive invention. I don't hold any ill will towards most non-despotic historical figures, but as far as I'm concerned Alex can get right in the bin.

Before you start complaining that the telephone changed the world in a very positive way, enabling family members to stay in touch when far apart and so on, I should state that my hatred of phones and phoning is pretty irrational and is based entirely on a severe phobia of using the things, so I may not be at my most level-headed in this section. But I should also point out that, increasingly, communicating over distance via the written word is overtaking the phone call. Millennials and Generation Z seem to have a distinct and powerful preference to chatting via WhatsApp rather than dialling a number, so it's not just the autistic community who would happily never pick up a ringing phone again. However, phone-phobia is certainly a common trait among autistic folks, and I'm going to attempt to explain precisely why this is.

First, it's very important to recognise that for a large number of autistic people phones are not just a source of anxiety and fear. It goes much deeper than that. Autism is a disability – this is something everybody needs to be absolutely clear about. Some autistic people may like to say it isn't, and to those people I say fair enough – it's up to the individual after all; but the reality is that to be autistic in this world, the way society works, is to be considerably disabled in a number of ways. Whether this is intrinsic to autism, or just a result of being in a world not designed for autism (the 'social model' of disability), is open to fierce debate, and I see strong evidence on both sides. Whatever the case, though, autism *is* a disability.

Not being able to use a telephone is part of this disability. There's something about the speed of discourse in a phone conversation that, together with the lack of secondary communication like facial expressions, can make successful communication really difficult. Autistic people often need more time to formulate responses and take in information – it's just how our brains work – and telephones simply don't allow for this at all. If you take even an extra second to think while on the phone, the subsequent micro-moment of silence discomfits the person at the other end. You can feel them bristle with irritation or confusion. Phone calls are like entertainment radio: dead air is a crime. And so we're buffeted into replying as fast as possible, and so we make mistakes or agree to things we shouldn't have agreed to. Every time I make a phone call, a period of perhaps a day afterwards is spent trying to unpick all the massive fuck-ups I've inadvertently caused myself.

But the disability goes way beyond this. Audio hypersensitivity is a part of autistic life, and it will continue to crop up as we meander through this book. Personally, I feel like my ears are out to get me, as they're so sensitive that they drag my attention from what I'm trying to concentrate on. If I'm reading and there's a TV playing somewhere within the house, my ears will diligently absorb every word they hear, transmitting this useless information to my brain in envelopes marked 'Very Urgent'. Whatever I'm reading has no chance of competing with that distraction. On the phone, the conversation I try to focus on is interrupted and blanketed by odd hisses and blips and pops, the tinny echoes of electronic communication. With this chaos in the background, I've no chance of fully processing everything that's said. This isn't 'phobia', nor is it anxiety – it's a manifestation of disability and as such, understanding and adjustment are absolutely vital. If I allow myself to recognise myself as disabled, then I'm able to see how relevant this is to me. I don't suffer from something as simple as 'phone-phobia' – I'm disabled by a genuine inability to make full use of the technology.

There's more to say about phones, however. Something that a lot of autistic people report when asked about making phone calls is that the act feels extremely intrusive. When I asked on Twitter, Hazel (@anlasair) noted that 'I sort of feel like I'm being rude imposing myself onto others ... I much prefer to text or email as then the person can just get to it when they're free rather than a phone call which is demanding attention now.'

This is something I feel in my very bones. I'm extremely sensitive to worries about bothering other people, for any reason. I'd rather die of thirst than ask someone if I can have some water. This is not a form of hyper-passive–aggression – it's a fear of disturbing other people's peace. I suppose this stems from knowing how precious my own peace is. Intruding upon a person feels unthinkable to me. Whether it's my own parents or someone working in a bank's call centre, I cannot bring myself to intrude upon their lives as strongly as a ringing phone does. It's just so *rude*! As a result, when a completely necessary phone call simply has to be made, I'll invariably spend a prolonged period of time before-hand trying to work out how to minimise my intrusion into their busy lives.

It goes without saying, I think, given that we live in a world where the new technology of constant access to the internet exists, that autistic people would generally appreciate a move away from the horror of telephones. Ironically, it's modern smartphones that provide the easiest means for this. Once complex bank transactions can be completed by online chat and all doctors' appointments are arranged by online form completion, then we'll be talking about a world better suited to autistic people – especially those of us who are non-speaking, for whom telephones constitute an unassailable barrier despite our possessing excellent writing skills. But we're not there yet. Too often we're forced to use our least favourite app on our phones – the call function – to talk to someone whose peace we often value more than our own.

AUTISM AND MEDICINE

There's a big problem in medicine when it comes to autistic people. Western medicine relies a little too much on a uniformity of human experience – it has to in order to function, on account of the costs involved and the number of people who need healthcare (basically all of us). Neurodiversity as a concept tips this up on its head, and muddies the waters considerably. The reality is that human experience is not uniform, not by a long way, and that autistic people in particular experience life, their health and their bodies in ways that may not fit neatly into nurses' and doctors' expectations. The problem is that autistic people don't get the healthcare they need, and this is something that contributes considerably to our lower-than-average life expectancies, often in quite unexpected ways.

Let's start with the process of an autistic person discovering something's wrong with their health. This part alone is fraught with difficulties. First, there's the issue of interoception – the ability to identify and act upon the sensations and requests made by a person's body. This sense is crucial in discovering that there's a problem, and it often doesn't work for autistic people. Some, for example, will fail to be notified by their body that they're hungry or thirsty. I have this problem myself – I never seem to feel thirst until it's extreme, and I can go a whole day without drinking anything, only realising at around 8 p.m. that I've a dreadful dehydration headache and a dry mouth. Similar issues can be found in

47

sensing the signals telling us to go to the loo, with predictably stressful consequences.

The most insidious presentation of this, however, is in the way our bodies communicate pain. Being able to tell our healthcare professionals what level of pain we're in is pretty useful. It seems to me that doctors kind of rely on this in order to make their judgements – after all, it's impossible to access the inner systems of a human patient in the way an IT technician can figure out what's wrong with a computer. Doctors and nurses rely on people to be able to say that their pain levels are, say, 6 out of 10 and for this to mean something.

Trouble is, ask me what my pain levels are and I've no idea. This is to some extent yet another example of interoception problems, but it's also a result of our erstwhile communication issues. I can't take the question at face value, and I find it impossible to be presumptuous enough to answer with confidence. After all, I don't know what 10 out of 10 for pain would be. I can assume I've never experienced pain that severe – for all my migraines and cluster headaches, I'm certain that someone else somewhere has experienced way worse pain than that. Without a frame of reference I'm lost, so the safest and most logical thing to do is hang around the average and say '5'.

The problem with this is that most doctors will immediately think, 'Oh, well in that case, it's not too serious,' and make a note that all is reasonably well. Trying to be careful and logical, avoiding being 'grandiose' or exaggerated, could cost us care that we desperately need, because unlike most neurotypicals we may be more averse to exaggerating or saying things that feel 'untrue' or 'inaccurate'. It may seem silly, but it's a real problem. The solution is either to get autistic people the world over to somehow ignore their aversions, or to educate doctors in these simple facts so that when they're speaking with autistic patients they know that subconscious understatement is a possibility, and adjust their practice and decision-making accordingly. I know which of these options is easier and more reasonable ...

Communication issues aren't limited to this one example, however. They go all the way through the healthcare process, starting with the absolute bane of my existence – telephones.

For reasons best known only to God, or Cthulhu, or whomever you subscribe to, British GP surgeries still seem to prefer to arrange doctor appointments via the time-honoured system of forcing people to make a desperate phone call the minute the surgery opens, hoping against hope they'll snag an appointment. It's as if the revolution of the internet, with its email and online booking systems, has completely passed them by. Although there are some surgeries where online booking is possible, or even necessary, phone is still king in the world of the NHS. When I asked the autistic internet about this, 500 out of just over 900 respondents said they were still forced to make phone calls to book an appointment; that's over half autistic people having no choice but to pick up the phone when they're ill. Many of them mentioned that they struggle to see their doctor for that very reason, with one person ('@Charliesays') saying that they actively avoid making appointments because of the stress of phone calls. All this is a result of ableism.

As we've just seen, it's known that scores of autistic people are petrified by phones to the point of avoiding ever using them. This is also absolutely known by everyone in the medical profession. As stereotypes of autism go, it's a well-known and unusually accurate one. And yet here we are, in 2022, still forcing them to make phone calls when they're unwell. It simply won't happen, and as a result autistic people all over the country and indeed the world may be missing out on vital care, because we cannot overcome the first hurdle. I once tried to set up the 'online booking' system at my own GPs, but failed because the first thing I had to do to establish this means of securing medical help without having to pick up a phone was make a phone call. As a result, whenever I want to speak to my GP – perhaps about a serious condition such as my high blood pressure – I have to make a phone call that causes my blood pressure to spike alarmingly, and usually leaves me with a migraine. This cannot be the correct way for medical care to operate.

Even if we do manage to overcome this hurdle, there's the communicative difficulty of having a conversation in person with the doctor at their surgery. I find this so stressful that I rush it, and find myself back in the open air having failed to ask three of the four questions that I'd carefully prepared. Just like all instances of communication, explaining a health complaint to a doctor is riddled with potential issues and opportunities for misinterpretation. Personally, I'm intimidated by the power imbalance that exists between doctor and patient, and I spend most of my time trying to ingratiate myself with them in the hope that this will encourage them to take me seriously. Part of this involves not taking up too much of their time, so once I have the first thing explained and out of the way, I feel unable to mention any of my other problems for fear of irritating them. In my case, I think this is yet another trauma response around communication generally, but it's very debilitating as I find myself either having to make a follow-up appointment – by phone – or simply moving on and hoping that the symptoms I wished to discuss go away on their own.

Honestly, it's a wonder that I'm still alive.

The problem is that doctors, despite their necessarily close proximity to developments in understanding neurology, are often just as prone to believing in the old stereotypes as anybody else, and the NHS doesn't have a very good history of providing cutting-edge training on autism (something that's beginning, finally, to change with the introduction of the new Oliver McGowan Mandatory Training in Learning Disability and Autism for healthcare professionals – look closer into the tragic story of what happened to Oliver McGowan, a young autistic man, to see how bad things had to get before real positive change was permitted). Many doctors simply don't know all that much about autism and the way that being autistic affects our communication and our ability to access medical care.

Personally, I think a few minor tweaks and changes could have huge ramifications for autistic people's health care: making email contact standard in accessing GP appointments would be an excellent start, and surely not beyond us as a technologically advanced society. Doctors who understood autistic people's communication differences and executive dysfunction would be a fantastic follow-up. Imagine if doctors were trained to ask if we had any other concerns in a way that didn't sound as if they were about to attack us if we were unwise enough to say, 'Well, there is one other thing …' If they knew that their autistic patients might be struggling to tell them everything, then perhaps they'd expedite that process by giving us more opportunities to share our other concerns, or have a system whereby we could write down our health worries while arranging our appointments. Why does everything have to involve speaking, after all? Are they not aware that many autistic people are either non-speaking or selectively mute?

If the NHS were to introduce electronic appointment booking as standard, with the capacity to enable us to write down why we need to see the doctor, in sufficient detail, then I'm confident that thousands of autistic people would finally begin to receive the healthcare that they have a legal right to.

But I'm just a guy who has no power to make this kind of thing happen, so in the meantime my recommendation would be that autistic people might want to try getting used to taking a companion into appointments with them. Having a friendly second person (a family member, partner or friend) to make the phone call and help you cover all of the necessary aspects of the doctor's appointment is invaluable – so long as you're in a lucky enough position to have a person like that available. Having that second pair of hands, eyes and ears in the high-stress environment of a surgery is incredibly useful, and for the time being is probably the best way to ensure the best outcomes.

I just wish we didn't have to rely on the kindness of others so much.

Perhaps, then, you might now understand how important it is to consider changing your expectations when it comes to communicating with autistic people and to be compassionate towards our differences:

- Be aware that we wear masks much of the time, and as a result we may be struggling with the conversation (and life generally, sadly) much more than you realise. Some of us are so expert at this that we manage to hide being autistic even from ourselves.

- Remember that wearing 'the mask' is exhausting. If you're part of the reason we're wearing it (i.e. because you cannot tolerate being around us *unmasked*), then it's worth reflecting on that ...

- Don't judge us if and when we mess up with small talk and those little extraneous bits of communication. If we overshare a little, is it the end of the world? If we're obviously trying to get away from the conversation, is that too much for your ego to bear? Be kinder, and realise we don't all like talking as much as you might.

- If we do have a meltdown, then follow these rules of thumb: back off, give space, reserve judgement. The last point is so important: don't contribute to the shame we already feel for losing control.
- Understand that our communication differences can have drastic outcomes, especially when trying to get healthcare. Be prepared to help 'translate' our experience to busy, uninterested professionals if you can.

2

AUTISM AND FRIENDS

THE EMPATHY MYTH

I first properly heard about autism at school. Not when I was a student – I often wonder what life would have been like if I'd been identified as autistic at a young age – but in my career as a teacher. ASD (autistic spectrum 'disorder'), as it's known in such circles, is something that comes up *a lot* when you teach. After all, the number of children being diagnosed as autistic has been rising rapidly now for many years. Many people, usually from a position of considerable ignorance, cite this fact as evidence of some terrible 'epidemic' of neurodivergency, suggesting that a nefarious *something* (famously the MMR vaccine) is causing this terrifying increase.

This is looking at the phenomenon from entirely the wrong angle. The truth is that our understanding of autism has developed in leaps and bounds since the early 1990s. We are now, as a society, far more aware of the fact that autistic people exist in all demographics. The revelation that girls and women can be autistic in considerable numbers – imagine! – has increased overall numbers hugely, as has a better awareness of autism in indigenous, Black and other marginalised communities. In such circumstances it would be strange for numbers not to increase.

It's common now for every class to have at least one autistic student, often three or four, so teachers have quickly begun to understand more about autism.

Or so you might think.

The unfortunate reality is that, generally speaking, autism understanding in education is pretty old fashioned and of poor quality. It's driven strongly by debunked myths and stereotypes, and struggles to keep up with contemporary theories and concepts. My training on the topic, delivered by non-autistic teachers and trainers, was therefore befuddled and riven with misinformation. Out of the many stereotypes on offer, the worst offender was the myth that autistic students don't have the capacity for empathy.

Empathy is an important part of being human. The ability to recognise and share the emotional experience of other people is a huge part of our shared society. And apparently autistic people don't have it. This isn't a niche or uncommon view. It's everywhere, and one of the most widely circulated myths about autism. The idea is that autistic children have no comprehension of the fact that other people have separate thoughts and beliefs, nor do they possess the ability to understand that others may be feeling different emotions from themselves. As a result, they behave awfully – in short, they're presented as self-obsessed monsters.

If you establish that a group of individuals lack empathy, then you're immediately prejudicing the rest of the population against them. Thoughts quickly turn to the similar media stereotyping of 'psychopaths' or 'sociopaths', who are often displayed as subhuman nightmares, despite both being neurological conditions. From there it's only a short jump to images of Patrick Bateman (Christian Bale) in his waterproof onesie in *American Psycho* or the terrifying eponymous child in *We Need to Talk About Kevin*. These are not fictional touchstones that autism deserves, and the continued spreading of the myth of unempathetic autistics will only make the situation worse.

The fact is that autistic people can and do possess empathy. Some have more than others, just like in the neurotypical community. Certainly, the form of empathy that deals with emotional and physical pain is often in abundance in autistic people. I cannot see a person suffering (for example a baby crying) without feeling intense sorrow and worry on their part, to the point where my absorption of the emotions of the moment can be debilitating. Autistic people regularly report feeling like 'emotional sponges' – upon walking into a room where some kind of conflict has taken place, we'll so frequently *immediately* take on board all of that negative emotion (some might call it the 'vibe' or 'atmosphere') that it can result in our having to sit down, or even bursting into tears. I've walked into rooms where it has been so obvious to me that the inhabitants have swiftly paused an intense argument, despite their smiles, and have walked out again feeling sick with the tension and misery in the room. It might not be identical to neurotypical empathy, but to suggest we have none at all is just plain daft.

However, as with all stereotypes, there are nuggets of truth in there – not enough to make it a valid proposition, mind – and it certainly is worth examining them. For all the *feeling* of emotion going on like a frothy, boiling tumult inside of us, autistic people very frequently don't *show* that emotion, nor do we quite know what to do with it. For example, there's a particular trait of autism (and some other neurodivergencies, such as schizophrenia) known as 'flat affect'. You may recognise it if I mention two similar concepts – 'poker face' and 'resting bitch face'. However, while poker face is usually a purposeful thing and resting bitch face has distinct negative effects, flat affect is a total neutrality in facial expression. No matter what's going on inside, the face will not reflect it. This can lead to the awkward situation where an autistic person may be absolutely emotionally floored by the sadness of a friend, but look completely nonchalant and unbothered. As I'm sure you can imagine, this might lead to some problems. Although flat affect is by no means universal to all autistic people – many of us are very expressive indeed, and I count myself as one of those – it's common enough to mean that you've probably met a few folks who display it.

And then, even if we do manage to show our sympathy for and understanding of your emotional state, we may have no idea what to do in support. This seems to me to be a common situation, and it's one that I recognise all too well. Feeling deep human empathy with a good friend or partner as they sob about some awful occurrence, I sit there awkwardly, kind of frowning, perhaps pursing my lips a little. It might be that the idea to give them a hug materialises in my head – though equally it might not – but I'm often so wracked with uncertainty that I never get around to doing it. Instead, like the character of Benjamin Poindexter in the *Daredevil* TV show, I rely on stock phrases that I know will work: 'I'm so sorry, that must be so hard.' Not because I'm grasping at straws for what emotional event is actually occurring – I get that – but because I just don't know how to respond; I'm lacking that part of the social script, in the same way I'm lacking the rules of 'small talk'.

There's another part of empathy that's very interesting, from an autistic point of view at least, and it's related to something called the 'theory of mind'. Generally speaking, this is a person's ability to recognise that other beings have their own thoughts, agency and emotional states – that they are, essentially, autonomous creatures separate from you and your particular thoughts and ideas. So, as an example, if I were to ask you to guess what I was thinking, as an autonomous being yourself you'd probably *not* assume I was thinking about exactly the same thing as you happen to be (i.e. 'Why is this strange man asking me questions, and where did he come from?'). Congratulations! You have theory of mind, and are consequently viewed as a fully fledged human being. Good for you.

Unfortunately, theory of mind has long been said to be missing in autistic people. Never mind that theory of mind is used as a standard test of sentience in animals, which raises uncomfortable repercussions when suggesting a human is lacking it – it's about as standard a concept in autism research, at least in the 1990s and 2000s, as you're likely to find. The assumption is based on bizarre research that I'd like to outline here, involving a story about two children who hide stuff. An autistic child is shown the situation in the tale – that one child hid one of the other child's toys in a bag while they were away on the toilet or whatever – and asked where the returning child would look for the toy when they realised it was gone.

Enough autistic children pointed happily at the bag (suggesting they didn't understand that the bullied kid didn't know the same information as the bully) that researchers loudly proclaimed that autistic people lacked theory of mind. The problem is that no further questions were asked, or possibilities pondered. No one asked, for example, whether the autistic child assumed that the child hiding the toys did this kind of shit all the time, so the other kid knew exactly where to look. Similarly, no one seemed to raise the fact that there was nowhere else in the little comic strip for the toy to be: the first child had come back, noticed the toy was missing, and, as they're in the middle of a vast white void, correctly figured it's probably in the damned bag sitting right there.

This serves as a great example of the kind of huge, broad conclusions that autism researchers (who've historically been overwhelmingly non-autistic) have been prone to make based on the loosest evidence. But the damage is done, and here we are in the 2020s still trying to unpick that damage from the reality of what it is to be autistic. For the reality, as I commented upon earlier, is that autistic people do have empathy. In fact, in quite a large number of cases, autistic people *seem* to be extremely empathetic, in ways that would be seen as quite unusual in non-autistic folks.

Many autistic people report having what we've collectively labelled 'hyper-empathy' – a kind of extreme set of emotional responses to people and animals in dangerous or upsetting situations. I mentioned my strong response to seeing children in distress earlier, but it's by no means limited to that. Other interesting features of this type of autistic empathy might include extreme empathy (and I mean *extreme*) towards animals. There's a reason why autistic people often have very strong views on animal rights, after all – so many of us seemingly cannot bear to imagine an animal in any kind of distress. For my own part, if I see or hear an animal in distress I'm immediately overwhelmed with anxiety and fear for that animal, and feel strong sadness and sympathy for its plight. Writ large, my worry about conservation and animal welfare is very intense and upon hearing bad news, such as the terrible loss of animal life in the wildfires in Australia in early 2020, I'm fairly likely to cry. This is not the behaviour of a person lacking empathy.

So, autistic people are as empathetic as they come. Sure, we've some interestingly varied and (to a non-autistic person) untypical ways of displaying empathy, if we manage to display it at all, but *it's there* for the majority of the autistic population. As such, any fears or doubts non-autistic people may have about the capacity for autistic people to form meaningful human relationships need to be assuaged – for the most part, autistic people are totally able to make friends, though it might be difficult for a variety of reasons.

AUTISM AND LONELINESS

It's usually assumed that autistic people are among the most introverted people on the planet, hermits in all but name, who would be perfectly content to live in a cottage on a remote island and never see another human being again. Now, this is admittedly true for some of us; my dream is to be able to retire to a Scottish island and live the life of a recluse, and no one's ever going to be able to talk me out of it. However, it's not as simple as that.

Some autistic people are, in many relevant ways, fairly extroverted. By this I mean they thrive on being with people and gaining attention (with the autistic proviso that they get downtime too) in a way that most non-autistic people may not expect. It may not look identical to neurotypical extroversion, but then nothing autistic people do is identical to its neurotypical equivalent anyway. The point is that the old and widespread stereotype that autistic people are anti-social, even misanthropic, is very flawed indeed. However, despite the fact that a reasonable number of autistic people would identify as being extroverted, many I've spoken to have reported that their natural extrovert tendencies have never been given the opportunity to blossom due to social anxiety, fear or the fact that they've been 'beaten out of them'. This may sound paradoxical, so let's look at it more closely.

Imagine an autistic child who's naturally extroverted. They're happy when they're with people, enjoy attention, even gaining energy from those around them. Highly empathetic, they thrive on company. Because they're autistic, however, they have a very different set of communicative skills compared with their neurotypical peers – all of the things I wrote about in Chapter 1. Over time, these differences in ways of communicating (presented as 'challenging' and 'difficult' by those around them) lead to problems: falling out with friends, arguments, being ostracised and even bullied. Gradually, this extroverted autistic kid is metaphorically battered by awful social experiences, so they withdraw and spend less and less time with people. For the rest of their life they're wary, cautious, even scared of social interaction, but they never stop being naturally extroverted. They're instead forced into a kind of involuntary introversion.

This is a story that has probably been repeated thousands of times across the world, leaving us with an autistic population that gives the appearance of being extremely introverted, quiet and wary of human contact, but which has within its ranks many, many people who would benefit from much more human interaction, so long as it's not *traumatic*. Sadly, we're a very long way away from living in a world that's comfortable and safe enough for these autistic people to get what they need – which is one of the reasons this book exists. So, if you know an autistic person it would be wise to assume nothing about our need for company. Autistic people *can* get lonely.

For now, the myth of autistic introversion endures, and sociable autistic people continue to be tarred by that brush, from school age all the way up to retirement. Autistic children at school, spending every lunch and breaktime alone hiding in the library or in some undiscovered nook under the stairs, are not seen as sources for concern. 'It's OK,' teachers may reason, 'they're autistic.' As such they fly low and under the radar, their intense loneliness eventually metastasising into something more dangerous – depression. I'm not saying this is a guaranteed conveyor belt, but it's a definite sequence of cause and effect that can so easily be missed on account of outdated ideas about what autism actually is.

If you wish to see the reality of autistic attitudes to friends and social company, find a group of neurodiverse students attending one of the more autism-friendly social clubs after school. In my experience, these extra-curricular groups (examples might be knitting or crochet groups, chess clubs, environment and animal welfare clubs, and tabletop wargaming societies) host a wide range of neurotypes, including autistic students, and it can be easy to see how some autistic people thrive on social contact: chatting about their interests, arguing about the finer details of their hobby, laughing, joking, sitting quietly together in companionship. This continues into adulthood, and I can say without hesitation that some of the warmest, most enjoyable social activities I've experienced have had a number of other autistic individuals involved in some way. The issue becomes more one of availability than anything else. Safe spaces, where autistic people looking for social connections can go without fear of being bullied or treated badly, are quite rare (despite being pretty much the norm in most areas of life), so finding one can take time and may even feel impossible at times.

Plenty of autistic people seek out friends. Many of us want friends, wish to spend time with them, get to know them really well. I have to qualify all of this with the eternal reminder that some autistic people are quite happy to go without friendships, but I'm increasingly of the opinion that these are the exception, rather than the norm. The rest of us are (shock, horror) similar to you neurotypicals, though the way we negotiate the winding obstacle course of friendship may be a little different from what is seen as standard.

SOCIALISING WHEN AUTISTIC

Autistic people online speak about a deep terror that lurks within, always ready to strike at us and truly spoil our day. It's an almost primaeval fear that hits us deep and always occurs when we're least prepared and most vulnerable. I remember the last time it happened to me. I was carefree, happy, enjoying myself as I sat with a friend, going over the most recent events of our middle-aged lives, drinking a beer in the sunshine. Suddenly, out of nowhere, it happened: someone else turned up and joined us.

Apologies for the melodrama, but how else can I communicate the horror of unexpected people at social events? Preparing for a social occasion is quite difficult for me, and it always has been. For many years I assumed this was a kind of introversion that I could battle and overcome, and I'd force myself to attend parties, gigs, meet-ups and so on very frequently. I now know that this was counter-productive; there's no 'overcoming' this aspect of autism, or at least not any way that I'm familiar with. The fact is that autistic people, even if extroverts in lots of ways (and it's surprising how many autistic people have extrovert qualities), have their batteries drained at an alarming rate by being around people, and a majority of us will often need significant downtime after, or even during, social events. Once I discovered I was autistic, I began allowing myself the time to go and have a lie-down on occasions where there was an expectation of socialising, and it has helped enormously.

It's therefore very important that autistic people plan and prepare themselves for these situations more carefully, taking this simple factor into account. Part of this planning will naturally involve knowing who's going to be there. I asked the large Twitter community of autistic people whether they preferred socialising with a single other person, or more than one, and got over a thousand responses. The clear preference (82 per cent) was to meet with only one other person, though comments made it clear that context had a big impact and that dealing with more people is easier if they're all autistic, for example, or if there's some shared activity like a game. But still, we like one on one, because it reduces the impact of all of those other issues I've already described. With just one person, there's only one round of small talk (or none if you know each other well), there's much less difficulty identifying your turn to talk, and it's much easier to gauge whether an attempt at humour or a change of topic will be met with enthusiasm or despair.

We plan and prepare ourselves for this one-on-one meet-up. As part of this we may rehearse greetings, go over relevant topics of conversation, work out where we want to sit (which may involve looking the venue up online and getting some good views of the seating plan – usually it's best to be tucked away, preferably in an alcove, or with our back to a wall) and so on, our sour experiences of socialising to date being warning enough that this kind of preparation is worth it. The thing is, many autistic people struggle with any kind of surprise or unexpected moment. I think it has something to do with our base level of stress being already so high. And so, seeing a third or fourth party appear to join our meticulously prepared-for occasion is absolutely heart-breaking and stressful. All of our careful planning, most of which was done internally, is suddenly rendered useless.

The likelihood of having to engage in awkward further rounds of small talk increases, as does the horror of trying to figure out when we're allowed to speak. Now, this isn't to say that all autistic people only ever want one-on-one socialising; there are plenty of us who like larger groups, especially if they're big enough – over four people, I suppose – to give the opportunity to hide away a little and recharge for a while whenever we need to. I've had pleasant evenings with a large collection of friends and acquaintances where, whenever I needed to, I could shut up and hunker down for ten minutes and no one batted an eyelid. But a dislike of unexpected additional people is as close to a universal autism trait as we're likely to get, in this chapter at least.

So, what's to be done? In this instance, the way to be more inclusive for your autistic friends and family is easy. Simply acknowledge the planning and preparation they're almost certainly going to be engaged in, and respect it. Don't throw any spanners in the works unless it's absolutely unavoidable. If you want other people to pop along, let the autistic friend know that this is on the cards! If you feel it's likely a third party might just appear, give them the heads-up. When about to meet up with an autistic buddy, try to take the following to heart:

- Don't change the location last-minute! This has thrown me off balance so much in the past that several times I've simply gone straight home – not out of grumpiness, but out of panic that I'm not mentally prepared for the new place. In worst-case scenarios, it might be I don't even know the new spot and I've never been there. In this case I can almost guarantee I won't turn up.

- Follow the autistic person's lead when choosing where to sit or stand. As with so many things I write, I'm aware how entitled and self-absorbed this might sound, but I ask you to try not to view it in a negative light: this isn't about preferences so much as it's about *needs*, and autistic people's needs are very real and the same as any other disabled person's requirements. The difference to, say, accessibility ramps, is that the autistic person's needs are more invisible, behavioural and easy to misinterpret as coming from an over-demanding, spoilt attitude, when they're anything but. So, as best you can, allow the autistic person to choose where to go as they will have needs that they will want to meet, whether they're to do with privacy, quiet, comfort, lighting or noise.

- Be cool if they get tired or want to leave earlier than you'd prefer. It's not guaranteed, but I find that when I meet friends my energy levels fluctuate wildly and there can be times where I flag so terribly that I have to suppress the urge to flee the situation. As such, abrupt endings to occasions have to be expected – it's amazing, and a testament to how much fun you are to be with, that we manage to stick around at all!

HAVING AN AUTISTIC FRIEND

It's fair to suggest that many friendships will in part be based on the autistic person masking out 'less desirable' aspects of their personality, which does cast a bit of a questionable light on such relationships, but frankly I'm so grateful to have some good friends in my life that I'm unwilling to press that point too closely.

Autistic people tend to have a very difficult relationship with relationships. Our communication differences are an obvious potential problem, as is our often-paradoxical introverted extroversion. We often simultaneously want friends, while wanting to get away from them as fast as possible too. We want to go out and spend time with them, but also desperately want to run home and hide in a cupboard to try to recover. The trauma we've suffered will always affect how we interact with our friends, but never make the assumption that because of that we don't want friends. As always, however, it's easy to see that friendships as autistic people see them are quite different from the neurotypical equivalent, which can lead to some conflict.

I spend rather too much of my day on Twitter, using social media to socialise. I say this with a completely straight face, as spending time on there, chatting to the people I know (most of whom I've never met in person) is effective socialising as far as I'm concerned. We share ideas, jokes, sympathy; we tell our stories, confide and advise. We just do it in writing and while in different rooms, towns, countries, hemispheres. I've no idea why this is viewed so disparagingly but it's obvious that the majority of people see this kind of solely online relationship as a pale imitation of the real thing, where you do all of these things while *sitting next to each other*. It's unclear to me how sitting next to one another is viewed as the absolute gold standard of friendship, but if you don't ensure you're sitting next to each other soon, you can write that friendship off, pal.

The importance placed on friends periodically sharing physical proximity is huge and bewildering. I suppose in the days before instant and reliable electronic communication, when the only alternative to sitting in a room together was the slow trudge of a postal service or, for more adventurous types, the intervention of pigeons, such a relationship would be pretty unfulfilling and frustrating. In the early years of the 2020s, though, where is the problem? Why are people so insistent that internet friendships are somehow lesser? Is it to do with touch? Well, I can safely say I don't believe I've ever touched any of my friends, save perhaps for a hug on their wedding day, and as a rule of thumb autistic people set little store by physical contact, preferring it to be only used with people we're extremely intimate with.

I believe it's reasonable to suggest that many autistic people have social circles that are primarily, if not entirely, online and that many would say that they have true, genuine friends that they've never actually 'met'. I also believe that these friendships are fulfilling and work (for us) just as well as 'traditional' geographically bound friendships work for neurotypical people. We don't appear to need frequent physical proximity in order to maintain our friendships, nor do we seem to need to be in as regular contact. I'm absolutely terrible at keeping in touch with people: I suppose it's a combination of social awkwardness and straightforward forgetfulness. This inherent forgetfulness that often comes with an autistic brain is frequently a problem – I can go for weeks and weeks so focused on a project or a worry or an interest that by the time I emerge and remember all of the people who are important to me, a year may have gone by and my best friend, sister and parents are all resigned to the fact I'm probably dead.

But autistic people don't seem to mind very much not hearing from you. If you have a friendship with a fellow autistic person, you can get away with having no contact for absolutely *ages* without the friendship really suffering. It's as if our friendships decay at a much slower rate than neurotypical ones. It often seems that you can forget to contact an autistic buddy for twelve months, and then happily message them and carry on the conversation you were having back then, without skipping a beat.

This is, in my opinion, an excellent feature of autism and I think it is, in part at least, built on a natural autistic ability to assume nothing and to not read anything negative into a lack of contact. When we're reasonably confident and happy in a friendship, there seems to be a tendency for comfort despite long gaps in contact, suggesting (and I'm veering alarmingly close to scientific hypothesis here without anything like the amount of data required to back it up) that this could be a natural aspect of autistic friendships. For our neurotype, friendships are hardier, sturdier, less prone to collapse and requiring much less maintenance. As a consequence, we're very likely to treat our neurotypical friends in this way too, albeit with much less success.

So, if you have autistic friends in your life (and I bet you do, whether you know it or not), it would be really good to bear in mind the following:

- They may not be as 'constant' as your other friends: they may come and go at random, are often silent and might be away for a long time, rather like a pet cat. This is not a sign they hate you or don't value you. It's almost certainly because the way friendship works is different for us.

- They may be perfectly content with a fully online relationship, and may not have much of a desire to 'meet up' somewhere. Again, this does not mean they despise you and everything you stand for; it's just that meeting up is hard work and basically unnecessary (as far as we autistic people are concerned). Better by far to enjoy the friendship as it is than to force ourselves into a situation where we may find ourselves under too much stress.

- They may seem to tire easily, rather abruptly shifting from being a core part of the social experience (possibly even the life of the party) to being distant and detached. If you do spend time together in person, they may leave the occasion suddenly, possibly without much in

the way of goodbyes. This is not a judgement
on how likeable you are; it's a natural result of
a social battery suddenly depleted.

I've left my friends without saying goodbye several times
in my life. One notable occasion was during a gig in
Nottingham, where my ability to enjoy the music and
being around lots of other sweaty, drunk people drained
away to nothing. Imagine an old mobile phone when
you try to do something complex with it: from 80 per
cent battery to 0 per cent in a few alarming moments. I
turned, pushed my way to the doors and stepped into
the cold night air. It was like jumping in a frozen pool
and woke me up immediately. I walked to the train
station feeling deeply guilty, but aware of the fact it was
necessary. Trying to say goodbye would have been so
extraordinarily difficult and fraught. I got home and
went straight to bed.

AUTISTICS IN LOVE

I mentioned in the last chapter that a very popular
Google search, if their predicted search algorithm is
anything to go by, is the simple question: 'Do autistic
people feel love?' I mocked the obvious nonsense of such
a question as hopelessly naïve but, when all is said and
done, this question is popular for a reason. It's time to
unpick that reason.

The stereotype of an autistic human is, as we've seen
time and again, a man who's awkward to the point of

hyperbole, desperately uncool, and fascinated by topics that would make anyone roll their eyes with boredom and disdain. This is the portrait of autism that we're shown day in, day out – the Raymond Babbitt model, I like to call it, as it's all so obviously based on the character from the 1980s movie *Rain Man*, as played by Dustin Hoffman. Ever since this film cemented autism in the popular consciousness, the Raymond Babbitt model has proliferated, almost to the point of gaining a life of its own. Nudged and aided periodically by non-autistic 'experts' on neurodiversity, it has spread and respawned endlessly, becoming the source of almost all of the most popular misunderstandings of what autism actually is.

The character of Babbitt is presented to us as wholly unsuitable for any kind of adult, romantic or sexual relationship with another human being. Childlike and naïve, he's a completely aromantic and asexual person. And as a result, far too many people appear to believe that all autistic people are exactly the same.

As far as we can tell, autism is primarily a genetic thing, and is therefore passed down from parent to child. Many autistic people, upon being diagnosed, report that they then realise how autistic their own parent or parents so obviously are. Similarly, when children are diagnosed, often at the behest of their school, it's very common for one or both of their parents to realise that they themselves have a lot in common and are autistic too (this is so commonplace that I seriously believe that any time a child is diagnosed as autistic, their parents should automatically be invited for a diagnosis themselves, just to speed up the process a little). People have retrospectively applied tentative diagnoses to their entire ancestry in response to discovering their own autism, based on their memory of how many autistic traits their grandparents, great-aunts and uncles and distant cousins have. It's often, it seems, a family affair. Now, none of this would be the case if autistic people weren't having sex.

Autistic people are human, and like all human beings the majority of us have the desire to enter romantic and sexual relationships. Autism does not strip us of that basic human need. Admittedly, there are plenty of aromantic and asexual people in the autistic community, but then this is true in the neurotypical community too. Autistic people date, and flirt, and sleep around, and settle down, and marry, and divorce. It's just something that's rarely discussed or considered by the wider public, mostly due to the twin stereotypes of the aforementioned Babbitt and the belief that autism is a thing that only affects children (as if we somehow 'grow out of it' on our eighteenth birthday), disconnected from the messiness of adult relationships.

Whole books could be written on the subject of autistic romantic relationships, and they probably should be. I intend only to address the basics here. However, it's worth bearing in mind that much of what I said about how autistic friendship differs from its neurotypical equivalent can also be applied to autistic romance. Perhaps autistic people are a little better suited to long-distance relationships, for example, for precisely the same reason that long-distant autistic friends seem to manage OK without spending time in close proximity.

There's also plentiful anecdotal evidence that autistic people are more likely to engage in non-traditional relationships. As is often the case, the 'traditional' doesn't really hold much meaning for lots of us autistic folks, and as such we seem to be happier to accept that we might prefer things that are decidedly non-traditional and be perfectly at peace with this side of ourselves. We know that the autistic population has strong ties to the LGBTQ+ community, with an emphasis on the TQ+, and I believe this is because our disdain for 'norms' means we're more able to exist the way we should exist, live the lives we ought to live, rather than force ourselves into the narrow definitions preferred by our great-grand-parents. Another example is the number of polyamorous autistic people, eschewing the norm and embracing something different that works for them.

One thing does seem fairly certain: when it comes to close, sexual and romantic relationships, issues such as sensory sensitivity and avoiding eye contact can fade. Whether this is a result of the vastly increased trust we tend to have in these individuals, or something to do with whatever 'love' actually is, I simply cannot say. However, I can say that romance can be … difficult for people who already have considerable issues with communication and understanding others' intentions.

I, for example, am hopeless at knowing if someone is flirting or not. I simply chalk it up to them being nice, and then around five to ten years later wake up in a cold sweat realising that they were actually coming on to me. It's important to note that in many of these situations I've been attracted to them too, and may even have been trying to flirt with them. I can give it, but clearly I can't take it. The problem is that it's a bit like an extreme version of that game of implication that I've already complained about: when it comes to establishing whether there's mutual attraction there, it all becomes this excruciatingly complicated game of signs and symbols.

For a collection of people who have an unfortunate tendency to 'overthink', it's an impossibility to painlessly navigate this strange, liminal space between fact and hope. Every possible flirtation might be explained by something else: perhaps they're in a good mood, perhaps they're drunk, perhaps they're in some way mistaken. And we sure as hell can't just go ahead and ask, bluntly, about what's going on. Even other autistic people don't tend to do this, which is either a good example of how we autistics absorb neurotypical social mores to our detriment or a sad example of how, when it comes to love, there's no such thing as clarity, no matter your neurotype.

Instead, we have to dance the impossible dance, and hope we accidentally get some of the moves right – enough, at least, to move on to the stage of the relationship before it all falls apart. But it does seem that despite this almost universal lack of clear and explicit communication, autistic people do seem to have success-ful relationships with both other autistic people and neurotypicals. It makes sense that autistic people would work well together, but this shouldn't be misread as 'all autistic people will get on with all other autistic people'. This would be oversimplistic nonsense akin to suggesting that all Scottish people are friends with each other. Autistic people have so much variation (just as you'd expect, being human) that intra-autistic relationships are not guaranteed to be perfect. In fact, even our autistic traits can clash quite alarmingly – as the autistic author Joanne Limburg said to me, 'One person's necessary stim can be another person's sensory hell.' As someone who has experienced this unfortunate clash first hand, I cannot agree enough.

However, despite this, it's reasonable to say that autistic people can make very good partners for each other. The shared experience of being different can be a hugely positive thing, as can shared special interests. Many autistic people on social media have talked about the joy of 'parallel play', where an autistic couple sit quietly indulging their special interests (of which much more in Chapter 4), separately but in the same space. Honestly, as romantic activities go, that sounds pretty blissful.

When it comes to physicality, whether its cuddling, kissing or sex, then the usual sensory sensitivity caveats tend to apply. After all, sex in particular is pretty intense when it comes to sensation, and it's easy to understand (I hope) that the sheer amount of touch involved might be overwhelming for an autistic person, and that's not to mention the ... ickiness of the activity. As someone whose sensory sensitivities are strongly triggered by temperature, humidity, sweat and so on, this is a bit of a problem when it comes to sexual activity – you know, the stuff they leave out of romantic sex scenes in movies, like 'sleeping in the wet patch' and so on – and it can cause further issues around libido, as it can be off-putting. For neurotypical people in sexual relationships with autistic individuals, it's good to be aware of how difficult it can be to balance the desire for sex with the dislike of some of the sensory aspects – there's probably always space for a fruitful conversation there that might make things more comfortable and satisfying for both parties.

Before we move on, a quick word about vulnerability. An interesting term I recently learned that has deep relevance to the autistic community is 'mate crime'. This is a term for abuse and mistreatment that's suffered at the hands of people whom we believed to be our friends, and it's unfortunately a common problem experienced by autistic people. It's where, for example, a person may twist their way into our trust only to cause huge problems later, whether financial by asking for money, or emotional by manipulation and abusive behaviour, or even sexual. Autistic people are prone to this not because we're gullible, but because we're often quite trusting, especially when people are kind to us.

'Mate crime' is not a specific autistic thing – it's a trauma thing. However, so many autistic people's lives are marked by intense trauma that we can safely say there's strong crossover. For so many of us, a kind-seeming person can often have a fast-track into our confidence, where they can wreak havoc – should that be their aim. If you have autistic people in your life, then I'd always recommend keeping a weather eye open and helping to vet new people. Don't be overbearing and patronising, but help be another layer of safeguarding. If you feel worried that any new people may have ill intent, then share that information. Be an extra set of eyes and ears for us, so we might have a chance not to get sucked into someone's unpleasant games.

3

TYING SHOELACES AND OTHER DAILY CHALLENGES

THE SPIKY SKILLSET

First one loop, and then the other. First one loop – why isn't it sticking in place? And then the other – but how does that work? How do I possibly manipulate these damned strings into that position? Push it through and tie the loop. These are just words. I give up. It can't be done and be damned anyone who can do this without drawing a sweat.

When I was eighteen I went on holiday to a beautiful corner of Slovenia with my family – a kind of last hurrah of childhood before galivanting off to university. As holidays go it was reasonably stress-free and enjoyable (for more on the autistic experience of holidays, see Chapter 7), and the food and drink were good and plentiful. But ask my parents about this particular trip and the chances are one of them will grumpily harrumph one word: 'shoelaces'.

As an eighteen-year-old newly invested in the world of indie music and its associated fashion, I'd come to an elegant solution for one of my most enduring problems. For years now I'd struggled with tying up my shoelaces. As a pretty capable teenager with good GCSEs and very high expectations for my A levels, I endured a kind of endless shame about the fact that I couldn't for the life of me maintain tied laces. I found (find, really – none of this has gone away) the act of tying them to be hopelessly convoluted and dependent on a long sequence of lucky chances: has each stage of the knot happened to mesh sufficiently for the whole to work properly? Are any superfluous knots in either lace – relics of past battles – in positions that will compromise the main knot? Are my fingers going to do as they're told today and not veer off into some esoteric adventure of their own? The whole thing seemed intolerable to teenage me, a wholly unnecessary gamut that spoiled every morning and the three, four, five times a day I'd have to kneel down and once again face the challenge as the knots fell apart uselessly.

I had worn Velcro trainers as a younger kid, but in my late teens there was absolutely no way I could get away with such an act of image self-vandalism. I mean, I was no king of cool (I collected miniature plastic soldiers as a hobby), but even I couldn't withstand the blizzard of ridicule that would ensue if I turned up in the sixth-form common room in lovely, comfortable Velcro plimsolls. But my newfound interest in guitar music and, crucially, the fashion that went alongside it (this was the era of the Strokes in the early 2000s) gave me a solution that, to my mind, was as beautiful as it was simple.

I would simply leave my laces untied. Perfect.

The wonderful nonchalance of scruffiness was to be my saviour. Admittedly, I now realise I had grossly misread the fashion cues in believing I could just let the laces of my black Converse high-tops hang free and loose, flapping around my shins as I walked, but at the time I felt unstoppable. At last I wouldn't have to face the daily ignominy of failing to do a task most five-year-olds can manage. I strode around the lake and town on holiday like someone who'd discovered a cheat code for life itself, with my parents trailing behind making apologetic faces to the German and Austrian tourists who glared at me as I passed. Over and over my father would ask, increasingly irritated, for me to sort my damn shoes out, and over and over I'd resist, protesting more strongly than I realised at the time.

The problem was that I didn't know why I found tying laces so difficult. I had no diagnosis of dyspraxia, for example – in fact I'd never heard of such a thing – and my diagnosis of autism was still fifteen years away. All I knew was that I was horribly deficient in this particular skill and that I felt as depressed by it as I did about my inability to catch, throw or kick a ball with any degree of competence. I couldn't help but blame these physical failures on myself and, if I'm honest, my nascent male identity was badly eroded by all of this. Being male at school in the late nineties was all about physical prowess. At the very least you had to be able to catch and run in a reasonably coordinated way. But this was beyond me, and ridicule was the natural result. Finding a solution to even a tiny part of this was liberating and there was no way I was going to give it up easily.

Autistic people are full of surprises, if people would only stick around long enough to discover them. Some of these surprises are the basic daily tasks we simply cannot do. Others are the overwhelmingly complex and difficult tasks we absolutely can do, and easily. The former are a source of extreme frustration for us – and also for those around us, who often have no real understanding of the reasons for our seeming inability to cope; difficulty with common tasks is a frequently cited reason why autistic children are viewed as 'difficult' by their school.

The autistic community has christened this phenomenon the 'spiky skillset', referring to the tremendous peaks of some of our skills, and the mortifying trenches of others. If you know an autistic person, then chances are they'll have a similar hedgehog-like set of skills with no apparent internal logic. It makes autistic people unpredictable, and hard to pigeonhole and categorise. It's a fundamental part of our existence and is possibly the one thing – more than any other – that causes us real problems when we try to interact with the world.

We may, for example, struggle to remember to feed ourselves while preparing to give a lecture at some prestigious establishment or we might find self-care like showering absolutely beyond our capacities while being excellent painters or dancers or analysts working on impressive projects. Or we might be totally unable to plan our days to the point of exasperation, and yet our social media accounts are exploding in popularity. Before I explain what impacts all of this have on our lives, let's explore in a little more depth exactly how one of these gulfs in ability works.

I began this chapter by admitting that I struggled to tie my shoelaces as a teenager. I still do, twenty years later at the age of thirty-eight. It's actually quite a common problem for autistic people. The reasons for this are varied. First, many autistic people are dyspraxic, a condition that leaves us absolutely at sea when trying to coordinate our hands, arms, legs and feet in any meaningful way. It makes many of us clumsy, prone to falling over, bumping our heads, poking ourselves in the eye, watching thrown balls sail past our flailing hands during PE lessons as the rest of the class laughs. It's a disconnect between our brain's intentions and our body's efforts, and while it may be comical to watch, it's depressing to experience personally. I can, however, play the guitar and am tolerably good at video games and painting the aforementioned little plastic soldiers – all of which require fine motor skills and tiny careful movements. So clearly dyspraxia isn't the full story.

A second reason is sensory, or at least it is for me. I hate shoelaces, physically. They drag on the ground, in the grime and the puddles and the dog poo, festering little tails of woe that we then have to carefully tease and manipulate into difficult, intricate patterns with our fingers – the same fingers we use for eating with – and we have to do this repeatedly. As a result I rush the job, desperate to avoid dirtying my hands any further. We already know how sensory issues can impact on an autistic person's behaviour (or at least we should, as I've gone on about it enough), and here that tactile fear leads to avoidance at all costs. Add to that the unpleasant sensation of bending over, knees and back all twisted, possibly augmented by the very common Ehlers–Danlos syndrome (a condition where joints and skin are far more supple and stretchy than the norm, causing considerable pain and discomfort).

Finally, there's something so dispiriting about knots. It didn't seem to matter how carefully I tried – they still slipped and slid loose and apart within twenty minutes. It was like I lacked some key piece of information, some vital step that would solve the problem. And actually I was. I'd reached the age of thirty-five before I learned, by way of a Reddit post, of all things (well, I certainly wasn't about to ask my adult friends for advice on the matter), that you had to pick the direction of your first loop more carefully – it had to be the lace that was tucked under the other in the initial, simple knot. Loop that one first, finish the rest and Bob's your uncle: a knot that wouldn't come untied the moment you stood up. I repeat that I was thirty-five. It's only slight hyperbole to say that this realisation changed my life; laces would now remain tied for more than a few seconds. You'd probably have to stop and think which loop you make first when you tie your shoes, yet you've probably done it the same way, without thought, thousands of times in a row.

So of course I hated tying my laces.

MONEY TROUBLES

If only it were confined to knots. Adulthood is a challenge that many of us autistics find ridiculously difficult. Seriously – the learning curve from the age of eighteen to twenty-one is so steep it's a wonder that anyone survives it at all. Many autistic people struggle to thrive in adulthood; so many everyday tasks are beyond us, and we lack the support to master them. Another common issue is an inability to manage our finances, often exacerbated by an inability to gain secure employment. Money is pretty important in this world of ours, and generally speaking autistic people find it difficult to secure and keep it, for a variety of reasons. Let's look at a particularly clear and painful illustration of this problem: free trials on subscriptions.

Let me take you back a few years to illustrate this. I've successfully navigated the confusing nightmare of early adulthood in the relatively safe harbour of Loughborough University, have somehow secured my degree, just about, and have opened three credit cards and secured a loan (on top of the standard student loan, of course) to help support myself. A steady income arrives in the form of a job at a fast-food place – at last I can begin accumulating cash rather than bleeding it – and I immediately sign up for a free subscription to a magazine. This in itself is something of an achievement as it involved making a phone call (we're years away from internet transactions) and sharing my bank details. I'd found my bank card tucked away behind my bed that morning, and was feeling confident I could handle the odd silences and terrifying lack of visual cues in a quick phone chat as I'd nothing else to worry about for the rest of the day. A clear schedule always helps me find the energy needed for these kinds of things. And so, one call later, I was the proud owner of three months' free subscription to *Empire* movie magazine.

The three months passed. A year. Two years.

Five years later I finally cancelled that subscription. I hadn't actually received an issue for over three years, however. By moving house but lacking the wherewithal to tell the subscription company (another phone call, which this time I couldn't face), I'd gifted someone in Loughborough a long free subscription, paid out of my empty, sad little wallet. I'd fully intended to cancel the subscription after the three months had ended – stick it to the man by claiming my free stuff and then strutting away like a boss, counting my cash. But life, and being autistic, had got square in the way.

I believe I lost something in the region of £300 in this enterprise – enough to buy a small second-hand car in those days. And this is only one example. I ran a poll on Twitter recently, in the spirit of scientific endeavour, to see how many autistic people had fallen foul of the 'free trial subscription' trap. Misery loves company, after all. The results were shocking but not unexpected. The vast majority of autistic adults (around 75 per cent of over a thousand votes) had similar anecdotes to tell, and the most common response to 'How much do you estimate you have lost' was £300 or more. Now don't get me wrong, the blame for this lies at the doorstep of those companies who use these tactics: after all, they know what they're doing and their reliance on people forgetting to cancel preys on the disabled disproportionately, in my opinion. But it's a very good example of just how granular the – seemingly – inconsequential difficulties faced by autistic people are; I wouldn't be surprised to find that many neurotypical people had similar stories, but not in the same quantity or so ubiquitously as the autistic community seems to have them.

And why does it happen? The most important reason is our deficit (and for once I'm happy to use this word) in 'executive function'. This is the set of skills that's responsible for planning, prioritisation, organisation – all the stuff that makes an adult human work properly. We autistic people have something a little … off in that department. It's as if someone forgot to instal this particular piece of software, so every other part of our brain is trying to do that work on top of its usual job, like a computer trying to run a new video game without the necessary graphics card. As you can imagine, this isn't particularly efficient and it goes wrong very frequently.

I often think how tremendous it would be if every autistic person were given a personal assistant to get us through this rigmarole – imagine how much would get done. But instead we find ourselves in a world of unpaid bills and forgotten appointments, losing money, time, important opportunities and even healthcare because a key part of our brain appears to have given up the ghost – we forget (in my case with comical frequency), we lose the energy to tackle them as they build up and up, and ultimately they become so seemingly unmanageable that trying to deal with them is just plain frightening.

A lifetime of messing up in this way can add up more than just financially. You become accustomed to being a bit 'hopeless', and it can reach a point where a vicious spiral occurs, a whirlpool of being a little crap at life. This can synchronise with depression (and the cause and effect of that relationship is intriguing, as we shall see later on) to cause real suffering, even homelessness. It can start with missing deadlines at work or a vital meeting with the boss. I remember mine started to really accelerate after I didn't attend an after-work training session. I totally forgot about it. I'd written it down and had it in my online calendar, but somehow just after each time I checked, something unexpected happened, which essentially wiped my short-term memory.

This happens a lot. I will, for example, be staring at my to-do list, notice that I have a thing I need to do very urgently in the next ten minutes, decide to do it and then bang – someone speaks to me, or I notice an interesting bit of pattern on the wallpaper, or a helicopter flies overhead, and I forget about it immediately, leaving no trace, no ghost of a thought behind. Before I know it it's six hours later, I'm hopelessly late with the task yet still blissfully ignorant of my failure as it's completely vanished from my mind. If I'm lucky I'll discover within a few days that I failed to do the thing. If I'm unlucky I'll not be told at all and my shameful tardiness will be silently added to the growing list of 'reasons to fire that guy'.

EXECUTIVE DYSFUNCTION

An accumulation of moments like this can destroy a life, and yet we don't often hear about executive dysfunction when we're diagnosed as autistic, and support for it ... well, it simply doesn't exist. In fact, for most autistic adults there's no post-diagnostic support of any kind. I remember the moment I was confirmed to be autistic ('Congratulations!') and the bemusement I felt as I was handed a modest stack of badly photocopied pamphlets titled things like 'So You've Just Found Out You're Autistic – What Now?' and 'Boy, Are You Going to Feel Weird Later On', all of which advised us to go to our local library to find further information. I got more helpful support the last time I switched home insurance provider (which, of course, was years ago – see above).

I left the hospital, my head swimming with a million unasked questions, completely adrift and confused. Luckily, I was already undergoing counselling for my severe depression at the time, so I at least had some assistance in a safe environment with unpicking what it all meant. But even then I felt as if I'd been dumped in a dark, unmapped forest and struggled to figure out what the hell was going on. The sad truth is the NHS offers no ongoing support for autistic adults unless they have comorbidities like learning disabilities – and even then the support is gatekept harshly and often unfairly.

And so we exist in a state of perpetual potential collapse, often only a few mishaps away from catastrophe. Rates of unemployment, homelessness and suicide among autistic adults are sky high – autistic adults are three times more likely to attempt suicide than the general population* – and I don't see how anyone can be surprised by this. Practical mishaps, compounded by a sense of being different and therefore not protected by social group dynamics, makes employment extremely precarious for many of us. If we do fall off the employment train, then homelessness becomes a true danger, and I cannot imagine a worse situation as an autistic person than not having a safe, secure refuge to call home. It seems that around 12 per cent of the homeless population in the UK is autistic – way more than even the highest estimated rate of autism generally. This means there are thousands of vulnerable autistic people without a place to call home, without a voice or any kind of representation – and how many of us were waved breezily from our diagnosis appointment with a useless stack of leaflets? As national scandals go, it's pretty dramatic.

But even if we do manage to hold down a job and stay in our home, we're still going to live in the physical manifestation of our disorganisation and stress. As such, recurrent life tasks like maintaining that home and – much more importantly – maintaining our health can be beyond many of us.

How many autistics does it take to change a light bulb? The answer is one – we're not fools – but we'll

* K. Kolves, 'Assessment of suicidal behaviors among individuals with autism spectrum disorder in Denmark', JAMA Network Open, 12 January 2021.

spend a year learning how to do things in the dark before we get around to it. Everything that goes wrong in my house becomes a learning adventure as I figure out how to live without it. The thing is, I'm savvy enough to recognise that the chances of me fixing the issue, or worse, having to get it fixed, are extremely low, so it makes good sense to learn how to do without the item or service in question. If the bathroom becomes unusable in some way – the ceiling of the room below begins to bow alarmingly due to unnoticed damp from the shower, for example – then you close off that room like it's radioactive, seal the door shut and forget about it, and make the best of the remaining bathroom, the one that's pretty much just a shower cupboard. If the ironing board breaks, just do the ironing on the floor on some towels or, better still, stop ironing altogether. If the oven stops working, stop eating food cooked in an oven and survive on a varied diet of beans and stir-fry.

Obviously, this is no way to live, and ignoring these issues is only going to lead to greater pain in the long run, but what choice do we have? Personally, I'm so limited in terms of energy that making each of these issues right feels impossible, and unless some kind of secondary support appears I've little choice but to find the workarounds. And as the house gradually falls apart around me, the spectre of the landlord looms ever larger and the threat of being kicked out shadows me all the time. Imagine this in thousands of struggling households across the country – hundreds of thousands across the world – and those homelessness figures begin to look even more alarming.

The good news is that there's much that can be done to help autistic people with these challenges. The practical difficulties are harder to resolve, but with some good-quality help with the practicalities and a proper display of empathy from those around us, this needn't be such a terrible experience. Let's take a closer look at the lace-tying issue. It's a problem to do with physical coordination, patience and memory – all of which are things we all occasionally struggle with, autistic or not. The difference is that neurotypical people, generally speaking, find tying shoelaces a walk in the park and have little sympathy for a person who finds them harder.

In fact, an inability to do something that's associated strongly with nursery school is perceived as being aberrant and somehow wrong – think a stronger version of the mockery of people who can't catch – and so we autistic people who do struggle get viewed as aberrant and wrong ourselves. This is frustratingly avoidable and eminently fixable, as all it would take would be an increase in patience, empathy and compassion. If your twenty-five-year-old friend can't tie their shoes, then (if I may be so bold) it's your incredulity, impatience and askance glances that will only make the situation worse and prevent them from figuring it out in their own time.

STICK TO THE ROUTINE

I've built up a strange atmosphere of superstition around a lot of my autistic traits – or at least a simulacrum of superstition, based on something much more prosaic. It's superstition without the supernatural, a recognition of the patterns and actions in life that lead to the best outcomes, and an earnest desire to repeat them – a 'stition', if you will. We're all familiar with the concept of 'lucky' items, for example – the professional athlete having 'lucky boots' that they always wear to competitions or a pair of 'lucky' pants that are associated with exam success.

As an autistic person, I have a long parade of terrible days and then occasionally days that are, on the whole, not too bad. Of course, I wish to attempt to sustain the 'not too bad' run as much as possible (the terrible days are just … well, terrible), and one way to achieve this is to limit those variables, keep doing the same thing, set up a strict and inflexible routine – some of which, to an outsider, would appear as arcane and peculiar as any old superstition.

Much has been written about the need for autistic people to maintain a routine, and how tremendously peeved we can be if the routine is broken. Often, it's framed as a way to project order on a chaotic world, or manage the enormous inherent stress of our lives, and I won't disagree – in fact elsewhere in this book these two mechanisms will be explored. But there's this other reason, one that I've been gradually coming to terms with over the last few years: that we seek to replicate success when we experience it, right down to the minutiae. That one good day, probably the first in months, becomes a model to repeat, to perfect if possible. I've found I will religiously repeat, as far as I'm able, every single part of a day in order to ensure it stays nice and positive, and doesn't collapse into the kind of disorder and horror that they all seem to have the potential for.

For example: I like to go for a walk every morning. As someone who inches across the tightrope of autism and ADHD, the need for a bit of regular exercise and energy-burning cannot be overstated, and the walk itself is a guaranteed way to improve my outlook and my day. But it goes further than that. I always begin my walk heading in the same direction – left, as I leave my doorway. To go right would, in my head and gut, be inviting catastrophe in a very similar way to how some would avoid walking under a ladder or placing new shoes on a table. But then things get even more comically convoluted.

Of course, I've walked pretty much every street and alleyway of my town – walking is also my go-to treatment for migraine and cluster headaches – so I've lots of familiar route options. As I walk, my internal satnav system judges each junction on how it has lately performed: has walking down Orchard Road helped recently, or coincided with positive thoughts or feelings, or been a feature of one of my rare 'good days'? If so, I'll invariably take that route. If not, I'll avoid it like the plague until at some point I associate it with positivity again.

I know that none of this makes a whole lot of sense, but I promise that, as far as I can tell, this is the automatic process my brain seems to follow every time I go anywhere. It means I'm interminably rigid in my habits as the alternative is to risk a Bad Day, and that's not something I take lightly. Take the walking issue – I'm fine if I'm alone and have no specific target to reach;

then I can wander to my heart's content. But if I'm walking with someone, then suddenly my freedom to jink around down whatever street feels nicest is curtailed, and I find myself having to tread paths associated with sadness, stress, pain or worse. It's no wonder, quite frankly, that I cannot abide walking anywhere with anybody.

Similarly, my everyday routines take on a tinge of ritual or ceremony. Everyone has a fairly standard morning routine of course – the classic 'shit, shower, shave' is testament to that, though why anyone would shave after a shower is beyond me. But how many of these people would fear their entire day is going to come crashing down if they accidentally or by necessity swap around the order a little, or, worse, miss something out altogether? If I miss a segment of my morning ritual – for example, the bit where I sit down on the living-room sofa with a coffee and check Twitter groggily – then I'll feel intensely uncomfortable for hours after, a similar feeling to knowing you've left the gas hob on and you're two hours from home, a kind of jumpy, extreme anxiety based on a fear that something truly terrible will ensue from your own foolishness.

Rigid personal routines are a feature of the autism folk myth the general public has absorbed. They're seen as almost endearing or quaint, although the reality is anything but. Our need for set, firm routines is stronger than most non-autistic people realise, and the penalty for deviation can be severe. There should always be a base level of respect for an autistic person's need for routine and an understanding of what underlies it. If a routine has to be changed, then compassion is required: an acknowledgement that this is damaging and a promise that it's being taken seriously. After all, if this chapter has taught you anything, it ought to be that the everyday existence of autistic people is a huge bag of stress, anxiety and discomfort, so at the very least you can give us this, can't you?

OVERCOMING INERTIA

It's said that Isaac Newton would often, upon waking up, sit on the edge of his bed for hours, unable to get up and get on with his day. The explanation given is that his head was so overwhelmed by interesting thoughts and conceits that it was impossible for him to budge past them, which certainly adds to the Romantic mystique of the guy, but it's also highly reminiscent of something that I, and many other autistic people, have to deal with on a daily basis.

I'm not in the business of 'diagnosing' historical figures as autistic. Suffice to say that there most certainly were autistic people in history, and it's highly plausible that some of them may have attained considerable levels of fame and fortune. A person like Newton (or Charles Darwin, Ada Lovelace or Henry Cavendish) may well have been autistic, but it's impossible to know for sure. However, there's little harm in recognising that some of these figures had traits or personality 'quirks' that are reminiscent of autism, and this particular habit of Newton certainly stands out.

His inability to move and get on with his daily routine seems very like the autistic trait that's often referred to as 'autistic inertia', which is one of those traits that – like executive dysfunction – is more likely to be seen as a negative rather than a positive in an autistic person's life. Autistic inertia is an inability to change task or focus – imagine a person totally wrapped up in doing one thing, like reading a book, who finds themselves incapable of putting the book down in order to go and make themselves a nice cup of tea. They want the tea, they're fine with the theory of making the tea and the book isn't necessarily gripping, but the required change of focus from the book's leaves to the tea leaves is just too much. The autistic brain is fully engaged in the one activity, intensely and even all-consumingly, and cannot easily retreat back to regroup and deploy itself on something else.

This can lead to the interestingly frustrating reality of one's body and brain actively working against your desire to do something nice and fun and relaxing. Because it's independent of any desire to do the other activity (unlike procrastination, where it's usually the case that the other activity is avoided because it's boring or hard), autistic inertia can prevent an autistic person from doing things that may bring them considerable joy. One example I've experienced all my life is an aversion to new things that, up until the moment of acquiring them, I've been very excited about. For example, there may be a video game that I've been looking forward to for years, obsessively tracking its development, decrying its delays and getting generally overexcited about the prospect of finally playing it. The big day eventually arrives and I have the thing in my hands and ... I suddenly have no desire to play it.

I always used to think this was just a kind of burnout, born of the overexcitement, but I now understand that what's really happening is my brain is struggling to adjust from one reality to the next. It is so hyperfixated on the hype and anticipation, with all that these entail, that it cannot adjust to the new situation of being able to play the thing. It takes enormous amounts of time and energy to switch focus as an autistic person. I've likened it in the past to turning circles for vehicles. Neurotypicals are able to switch tasks as easily as a car can make a U-turn. Autistic people, on the other hand, seem to make U-turns at the same pace as an ocean liner, requiring huge amounts of patience.

Given enough time, my focus will be able to shift and drill deeply into the game, probably playing it for hundreds of hours, but only once my attention has undergone this ponderous, gargantuan about-face. This attention-switching delay occurs in all areas of life and can be one of the most disabling aspects of autism. The problem is that it's too easily mistaken for the aforementioned procrastination, or even pure laziness. To an uninformed outsider, an autistic person's inability to move between different focuses can seem a terrible character flaw. Rather than seeing it as a central part of the disability that is 'autism', it's seen as evidence that the individual is a feckless loser, impacting on relationships, employment and more.

Autistic inertia is a very internal thing, and it's hard for others to actively assist autistic people through it. A simple understanding of the nature of inertia, however, together with oodles of patience, can go a long way towards giving autistic individuals the space and time they need to navigate changing tasks and focuses. Actually stepping in and directing autistic people, telling them to 'now do this' or 'now do that', is almost always doomed to failure, unless the two of you have an excellent relationship. After all, as you will see in Chapter 8, many of us have a distrust of authority that includes a dislike of orders. On top of this, though, there's the issue of pathological demand avoidance (PDA).

This intriguing possible 'feature' of autism (or possibly ADHD – it's very unclear where exactly PDA falls) is heavily discussed online and has whole groups set up for it, and even a charity, although it isn't currently accepted by all within the medical establishment and only some doctors are happy to diagnose it (which itself is a pretty peculiar state of affairs). As such, it occupies an incredibly controversial spot in the world of autism advocacy, with some autistic folk certain that it exists and others who are equally adamant that it doesn't. I fall slightly into the first camp, primarily because I recognise so much of myself in its traits, but I have to acknowledge those who are unconvinced. On top of this is the issue with its name: 'pathological' divides autistic people. We spend a lot of time reminding neurotypical people that autism isn't a disease, and then we find a possible key trait labelled as exactly that. Suffice to say, then, that I write this short section of the book with particular care and ask that it be read in a similar vein.

PDA is the name we give to a set of behaviours that orbit the idea of 'demand', referring to any kind of request made by someone else of the autistic person in question. The term 'demand' is impressively vague here, running the gamut from direct order, barked as if by some drill sergeant, all the way through to friendly and gentle reminders, perhaps from a friend you love dearly and would wish no harm to. You see, it doesn't matter: whatever the 'demand' is, and whoever it is from, the reaction will be the same. An immediate and often extreme kickback, akin to when the mule in *Buckaroo!* finally snaps under the increased weight of plastic nonsense you have piled upon it. The moment the request is heard, the reaction is a total refusal.

As you may imagine, this is not an easy trait to live with – take it from me … I was asked to open the kitchen window this morning and it totally ruined my day. It affects almost every part of life that involves other people, from romantic relationships to work to school to random interactions with strangers, and it's very visible. Indeed, considering that autism is still generally referred to as an invisible disability, there are parts of it that are undeniably easy to spot, if only people knew what they were looking at.

It starts with the request, of course. If we take something trivial by way of example, it will better illustrate the phenomenon, so let's suggest that the request is for me to take a shower. Now, in the spirit of full disclosure, I truly enjoy showers, and find them tremendously relaxing and generally good for the soul. Moreover, the feeling of freshness afterwards is something that's hard to replicate. With the right water pressure and a nice fluffy towel, a shower can be as close to paradise as I'm ever likely to get. However, if anyone (and I mean 'anyone' quite sincerely) ever dares suggest to me that I take one, for whatever reason, then I can guarantee that I will not be having a shower that day. It sounds ridiculously contrarian, and I understand that. And it is, in several ways. But it's not voluntary and it's not a choice. It's as instinctive a kick against the requester as the flick of the lower leg in a reflex test. Just as I cannot stop my leg jerking around melodramatically when the doctor taps my knee with his tiny hammer, it's impossible to resist the urge to refuse point blank to do what I've been asked to do. This has the unfortunate result that even though a shower would probably be the best thing for me at that moment, my brain will fight to avoid ever being told what to do and simply will not let me take one. This stands even if I was already planning on showering only a few moments before: the request or demand made overrides this, and I find myself refusing something I was perfectly happy to do.

I must sound absolutely insufferable to you by this point, and the sad truth is that PDA is very difficult to live with, in every sense. The instinctive kickback can be fought and ignored, with practice, and I think a number of adults do master this, but the internal fight remains as my reasonable side battles with this angry, unreasonable bit of my brain. Even when I do succeed, I find my brain's 'bandwidth' narrows at these times, leading to loss of temper and general irritability whenever anyone asks me if I'd like a cup of tea.

It's from all of this horror that the 'avoidance' in the term 'PDA' emerges. When a person has to deal with this relentlessly negative chaos whenever a demand is made, it's natural that they would seek to avoid these demands in the first place. Someone with a PDA profile (like myself) will therefore expend enormous amounts of energy and social capital to ensure that no demand can ever be made of us. This can be a positive, if it leads to me taking the initiative and getting things finished before I'm even asked to do them – and when I manage this, it is a joy that can rarely be matched – but it can lead to a cycle of negativity that leads to isolation, as I fail to cope with demands made of me and retreat further into myself, making myself as unattractive to potential enquiry as I possibly can be. After all, if I manage to alienate everyone in my life, then presumably the demands on my time and attention will dry up, yes?

As subconscious coping mechanisms go, this really isn't great.

I believe that PDA and autistic inertia are closely related, and possibly even different manifestations of the same thing. If inertia is the force gluing us to whatever we're hyperfixated on at that moment, then PDA is the natural end result when we throw other people into the mix. An autistic person will have their issues around changing tasks and changing focus, but will eventually manage these on their own terms (with care and a peaceful setting, ideally). Interrupt that slow, gentle process with an external question, demand or event (a partner asking for something, a phone ringing, a knock at the door), however, and all hell breaks loose internally. That slow process, the cruise liner turning about – as pains-taking as carefully untangling Christmas lights in early December – is suddenly broken. Our hyperfocus is disturbed and our mood follows a predictable path. The result is likely to be anger, irritation, despair or actual pain; the social relationship with the person making the demand is tarnished and possibly broken, and the cycle continues towards desperately trying to avoid that situation ever, ever happening again. PDA as we know it is born.

I want this book to be as helpful as possible, but when it comes to PDA profiles (whether you believe in PDA as an actual diagnosis or not) it's difficult to provide solid advice beyond the basic 'be gentle'. Frustrated parents and teachers often get in touch with me to ask if I have any advice on how to help students who *appear* to be PDA, and really all I can say is 'be mindful of the hyper-focus'. Asking an autistic person to change task abruptly, without warning, is a sure-fire way to meltdown, and just providing gradual, incremental warnings that the change in task is coming up is helpful.

Imagine it like a motorway junction. There's a good reason why these don't just suddenly appear out of nowhere, as this would lead to unimaginable disasters. Instead, drivers are warned at intervals that the junction is approaching with a succession of signs – 'Junction 9 in 1 mile', 'Junction 9 in ½ mile' and so on – and even then, there's still the funky and weirdly exciting countdown that we get on British motorways (\\\ … \\ … \ … BLAST-OFF!) as we make that final approach. And *even then*, the junction itself is a gentle and serene slight change of direction, rather than an abrupt 90-degree angle littered with crashed cars. Treat autistic people's task-changing as a motorway intersection and I believe you'll see much happier autistic people.

As you're probably beginning to understand, the problem here stems from a lack of understanding of what autism is: after all, how can you offer to help someone whose difficulties you don't comprehend? But once that understanding is there, the next steps might be:

- Offering to help with some household admin (or even cancelling some of those pesky subscriptions).
- Maybe a little more time spent explaining the art of shoelace-tying to autistic students of all ages. More practical help can be offered to autistic students and adults, though it needs to be offered with respect, without patronising us or making our feelings of shame worse.
- And ultimately there also has to be the understanding that it's OK for us autistics to refuse that help; after all, we have our personal pride and desire to be autonomous. But how nice it would be to have the opportunity to turn down a kind offer of help!

Perhaps we can start a sea change in how autistic adults are viewed – not as incapable and hopeless, but nor as absolutely fine. We have our spiky skillset, and as such there will be aspects of adult life that we find difficult, despite our successes.

4

MORE THAN A HOBBY

HOW SPECIAL IS A 'SPECIAL INTEREST'?

The word 'special' has been buffeted about for the last few decades. It's got to the point where I'm always genuinely confused about what its connotations are whenever I use it. In the 1990s it felt like its use as a term to replace 'disability', especially in the UK, was going to cause it to become increasingly pejorative, used more and more as a scathing playground insult. But it never quite seemed to fall into that trap, although ghosts of this connotation do remain. We need to place all of this to one side, however, and treat the word as unencumbered by these nuances as possible. So when I speak of 'special interests', and I will use the phrase a lot from now on, I mean special as in 'better, greater or otherwise different from what's usual'.

Most autistic people have special interests. This phenomenon is one of the great universals of autism, so much so that it seems to bleed into other neurodivergencies, such as ADHD. They are interests that are of huge importance to us, that seem to take up more space in our heads than regular hobbies do for neurotypical people. They are felt intensely, experienced with a passion veering on obsession, and are never far away from the forefront of our minds. They seem to nourish and sustain us, and can feel (to me at least) important enough as to give my life meaning at times where everything else seems hopeless. In short, special interests are important and they're widespread, meaning that they're one of the better-known traits of autism, although, as we've seen time and again, much of this is tainted by simplistic stereotype and assumption. So, let's start there.

The stereotype of autistic special interest is trains. There's no two ways about it: for whatever reason, this particular method of transport is the number one cliché. It's so deeply embedded in our popular culture's view of autism that it forms part of the unhelpful archetype of autism: the cis white boy who plays with toy locomotives. And while there are plenty of autistic people who do love trains (I'm one of them), there are millions who can take them or leave them. As splendid as *Thomas the Tank Engine* is (strange hyper-colonial/mega-capitalist messages notwithstanding), liking the book and collecting the toys are far from a universal trait of autism.

Autistic special interests are almost as varied as the autistic people who spend every available moment thinking about them. There's no limit to them. They can be quiet, individual, thoughtful in nature, or they can be physical activities involving other people. Special interests of autistic people I know in real life include topics as varied as *Buffy the Vampire Slayer*, the Beatles, building gaming PCs, submarines, street dancing, cows, *Sonic the Hedgehog*, and cooking desserts and pastries. Despite the vast diversity of interests, however, there are lots of commonalities that are shared by autistic people all over.

First, these special interests help us regulate our moods and manage our stress levels. This is an extremely important aspect that's all too often overlooked.

Second, they help us find and maintain social groups to be a part of, whether in the form of clubs, fandoms or societies. For a group of people who can struggle to find ways to interact with others, this is an invaluable benefit.

Third, they frequently (though not always) form part of our way to support ourselves. Thanks to the almost inevitable fact that we will become pretty expert in whatever topic it is we focus on, being able to make a little money out of our interests is entirely possible, and some autistic people have managed to forge entire careers based on them.

My special interests are reasonably well documented, given that I've written a whole book about them (*What I Want to Talk About* – by all accounts it's worth a read), and it's not my intention to go over them again in detail here, despite the urge to share all my loves and passions being almost overwhelming. Instead, I want to discuss how these interests work, and how important they are to autistic people. Any references to LEGO or *Minecraft* will be entirely incidental and by no means a permanent written record, symbolic of autistic people's absolute need to talk about our interests ...

A CALM PORT IN A STORM

Our lives of stress and anxiety can cause tremendous problems for our health. It's sometimes asked what an autistic person without chronic trauma and its associated stress would be like, an autistic person who has somehow avoided experiencing a lengthy litany of stressful social miscommunications, and managed to negotiate school and family life without being bullied or ignored by person after person. I'm not sure I can imagine it, as it feels so alien, though I'm sure some people like this must exist.

There's a very real likelihood that much of what we see as 'autistic behaviour' is simply a collection of ordinary responses to prolonged and repeated traumatic moments. It's a harrowing thought, and one that has kept me up at night many times. But whatever the outcome, this continued trauma, brought about by serious communication difficulties and sensory sensitivity, can leave many autistic people prone to moments of very intense fear, anxiety and panic over the course of an average day. When this fog of stress descends, it's vital to have some kind of safety net to collapse into. This is where special interests come in.

I had this happen frequently when I was teaching English at a secondary school. Every single lesson I would panic about the class about to be in front of me, worried time and time again that I was somehow incapable of doing my job, despite all the evidence to the contrary. In these moments I'd find myself resorting to what was probably my best tactic: opening Wikipedia and reading as quickly as I could some information about steam locomotives from the 1950s. Reflecting on this now, it's incredible how effective this very simple technique was. Somehow, reading up on the wheel arrangements of various ancient, polluting, steel behemoths calmed me down much like I expect a lovely massage would calm down anybody else (personally, I can't abide any kind of massage due to my absolute intolerance of having to lie on my front, prone and vulnerable, while a stranger pummels my spine). Even if pressed, I couldn't truly explain why this particular subject helped so much. The only reasonable explanation I have is that these trains' status as a special interest somehow did the job.

It would only take a few moments to calm down in this way, and afterwards I would be able to deliver a lesson perfectly well, to my usual pretty high standards. However, I was forever petrified that somebody in management would look into my internet history and wonder why on earth I was spending so much time reading about A4 Pacific locomotives, when I should have been teaching Year 8 about apostrophes. I suppose this is a big part of the problem: we autistic people find little workarounds, tricks and bespoke solutions to our personal difficulties. Yet these are often ever-so-slightly odd, meaning that when neurotypical people spot us in the act they may assume that we're up to no good, in that peculiarly pessimistic way that they have.

My experience of reading about my interests in order to calm myself down is shared by many in the autistic community. Special interests seem to be both an inherent trait of autism, but also an excellent coping mechanism to help us handle the stress and anxiety that being autistic in this hostile environment generates. In the past I've compared it to various things, from taking a warm bath, to hiding inside your own brain or even hugging, to tickling your own brain. For me, at least, it's a strangely physical sense of comfort and respite, like a contented yawn or feeling pleasantly full after a nice meal. In allowing myself to be absorbed in a topic I'm deeply invested in, I seem to purge my neurons of whatever fear was overcoming them. I honestly couldn't do without what special interests give to me.

I use my special interests as a haven, a place I can go to when everything else seems too stressful. When I was a child my LEGO and video games were where I hid from a difficult home life. My parents had a bit of a rough time in the 1990s, mostly because of the recession that hit hard in 1991 or so. Lots of lost jobs later, we ended up staying with my grandfather in a living arrangement that wasn't entirely conducive to calm and peaceful serenity. As a result, my bedroom was a haven where I could completely immerse my brain in whatever my newest obsession was. I had a lot of LEGO, usually all spread out on the floor in a kind of cityscape, with a police station, fire station, harbour and tropical pirate lagoon – you know, the standard urban sprawl. I would concoct detailed, intricate narratives that would allow me to disconnect entirely from the pressures that haunted the rest of the house, with jailbreaks and huge fires and pirate-related shenanigans. Whenever I exhausted this particular mental 'panic room', I'd switch on my Sega Mega Drive and inhabit some other fictional worlds for a while. Sonic the Hedgehog's green, pleasant lands were a favourite, as was the strange, colourful world of Mickey Mouse in *Castle of Illusion*. Unlike a general, ordinary gaming hobby, where completing games and getting high scores are the aim, this was fixated on the worlds themselves. I would spend hours exploring them, even wondering what was beyond the playable levels, what lay beyond the trees in the background, what sights were hidden from view.

Obviously, even then my 11-year-old brain was well aware there was nothing else there – with video games all you get is what's programmed, there's no extra unseen element to the tracks on *Super Mario Kart* – but I didn't care. I lived to imagine the wider worlds of these games, seeing them as a true refuge. This has never gone away. These days the game worlds are much more developed, open and free. You can wander to your hearts content on a game like *Red Dead Redemption*, and I do. Frequently. Similarly the world of *Minecraft* offers an amazingly varied and enjoyable safe place, to such an extent that I've quietly developed and built a whole world over the last decade or so, filled with cities, villages, castles and landscapes, all for my own enjoyment and as a place to go when the difficulties of real life get too much.

I think this type of escapism is a big part of why special interests are such a feature of so many autistic people's lives. It would explain why fictional settings, in TV, film, literature and games, are so enormously popular as subjects. A good friend of mine tells me that she has a well-developed fictional world tucked away in her head where she can escape to when the stresses of life get too much, and that this is at least partly based on various fictional worlds. It's certainly the case for me. These locations become something we deeply care about. Even today I remember the levels and music of my *Sonic* games and the aforementioned *Castle of Illusion* – to the point that you'll often hear me whistling the tunes while I make a cup of coffee – and very often, as I lie in bed trying to get to sleep, I'll reimagine exploring those places, my memory of them as rich and fresh as when I was twelve, and before I know it I'll be sound asleep.

From Marvel comics to the world of *My Little Pony* or *Breaking Bad* (and who'd ever expect those two universes to be mentioned together in a sentence – imagine a crossover), these rich, detailed fictional worlds are perfect settings for autistic people to get lost in and find peace and quiet. But there's more to interests than just make-believe spaces.

A key feature for many autistic people's interests is collecting. Now, again, collecting stuff is not uniquely autistic – plenty of neurotypical people collect stuff, after all. Nor is it a feature of every autistic person (nothing is, remember?). Yet it's unusually important to so many of us. It's very common to see the collection of a fairly esoteric type of object. Perhaps rocks, or beermats, or flags, or insects, or Barbie dolls, or socks, or model trains, or playing cards, or cardigans, or ... you get the idea. If it can be collected there will probably be an autistic person who collects them.

Then there's Pokémon.

Collecting these colourful little monsters has been a favourite interest for so many autistic people since the late 1990s, when the original games first appeared on the Nintendo Game Boy. It's fascinating to speculate why this particular franchise is so overwhelmingly popular with autistic people; I think it's the combination of the collecting and the data-heavy numbers game that the monsters themselves represent.

If I may go into a little more detail, all Pokémon, whether in the main series of games or in the mobile-phone version *Pokémon Go*, have statistics that determine how strong they are, and understanding this can get very deep indeed. Though it is a myth that *all* autistic people love numbers and maths, it's not entirely divorced from reality: many autistic people enjoy the security and fixed nature of numerical data, and Pokémon provide this in spades. Finding the little beasts, judging their strength and how they will fare fighting other little monsters, and building them up into lean, mean fighting machines is an experience that really works for a lot of autistic people: it provides lots to think about. It allows for plenty of what we call 'theory-crafting', whereby we daydream about good attack combinations and how best to organise our Pokémon – something I've always found very useful in boring meetings or on long train journeys when I need a way to profitably pass the time. Figuring out that a combination of ghost and psychic type moves on a fully powered-up Mewtwo will make it essentially unbeatable in competitive play is, quite simply, fun – as well as being an achievement of sorts.

This is collecting with a purpose – collecting interesting rocks never had the option of making them fight each other to the death, after all. On top of this, playing the game provides a safe, manageable means of socialising, where we can meet up with other similarly obsessed individuals and play together.

This particular kind of special interest is very common among autistic people, and it is not limited to Pokémon. Similar pursuits that scratch the same itch are tabletop wargaming, like *Warhammer* – you know, the game played with little miniature soldiers that have been painstakingly painted. These games are, at their heart, a beautiful combination of collecting models and figuring out their numerical statistics. Then there are massively multiplayer online games like *World of Warcraft* or *Elder Scrolls Online* or even *Grand Theft Auto Online*, all of which fulfil the same kind of aims and provide the same comforts and detail that so many autistic people thrive on. It may come as no surprise that all of these have captured my interest at one time or another.

Collecting things is a long-term joy, and one that feels forever productive. It gives us focus and goals, and knowing our collections in detail, whether it be the age and origin of our collection of rocks and fossils, or the speed and endurance of our collection of electronic sports cars in *GTA*, is a source of pride and tremendous satisfaction, once again enabling us to find a calm place to inhabit in the maelstrom of the world.

Beyond the need for a place to hide and recuperate, special interests enable us to focus our brains in a strangely pleasurable way. When the constant demand of looking at the 'big picture' in life gets too much and too boring, the ability to tweak our brain's lens to precisely focus our laser-like attention on something specific is a wonderful feeling, rather like it's allowing our brain to do what's natural for it, rather than expecting it to cope with the wide view, which can feel so ... false. This is no wonder, if you subscribe to the concept of monotropism.

MONOTROPISM – THE ATTENTION TUNNELS

In 2005 a new piece of research, led by Dr Dinah Murray, was published in the scientific journal *Autism*.*
It had been gestating for a number of years through the late 1990s, and would go further than possibly any other theory or research to provide a 'grand unifying theory' for autism and, potentially, ADHD. It detailed a new way of considering the autistic brain, centred upon the concept of monotropism. The word, from the Greek for 'single turn', refers to the way autistic brains seem to be built to focus attention on single parts rather than the whole, or to put it another way, the predilection for autistic people to struggle to see the wood for the trees, or indeed *a* tree. Monotropism posits that autism is inherently to do with narrow focus, and it can be applied to almost all aspects or traits of autism, from our sensory sensitivity (a single focus on a particular sensation, driving us to distraction) to our communication difficulties

* D. Murray, 'Attention, monotropism and the diagnostic criteria for autism', *Autism*, 9(2), June 2005, pp. 139–56.

(a single focus on word and phrase meaning causing issues with implication, connotation and such). It also very neatly explains how autistic special interests operate.

Sometimes, autistic special interests are *extremely* specific. I've heard of an individual who had a deep fascination with the masks that plague doctors used to wear – those long, beaky things that haunt the dreams of many of those who have studied the seventeenth century; another acquaintance of mine on Twitter has an interest in watch straps, with particular focus on how the colour of the nylon on certain types affects the fit, by changing the chemical and elastic properties of the material. This is not unusual. Often, broader interests will home in on smaller foci, which can become of great importance to us. There's comfort to be found in the minutiae of life, something that I find whenever I give myself the chance to really zoom in on things and study the intricacies. Perhaps this is why miniatures of all kinds are very often popular with neurodivergent folks.

Monotropism as a theory helps us to understand why this is so often the case. We autistic people, as Dinah Murray's son Fergus pointed out to me, 'tend to concentrate our attention (or processing resources) on relatively few things at a time. That is, where most people are polytropic – meaning that they have multiple channels of processing going on, or multiple interests aroused at a time – autistic people are monotropic, having our attention fully occupied by a small number of interests at any moment.' As a result, we're able to devote enormous energy and time to singular focuses. We approach the world like laser beams, I suppose, rather than wider car headlights or floodlights, with everything within the narrow focus of our attention drilled down into its very depths.

And this doesn't just apply to our interests. According to Murray, 'Neurotypical social communication generally involves multiple channels of input and output, which people are expected to attend to simultaneously: not just words, but tone of voice, facial expressions, body language and eye contact. Most people are capable of juggling all of these, going in both directions and often with more than one person at a time, without consciously thinking about most of them, and bearing in mind all sorts of social context, like power relations, at the same time.' It's easy to see how this could prove to be an extremely effective explanation for much of what I described in Chapters 1 and 2.

Murray even contends that monotropism could well stand behind autistic sensory sensitivity, suggesting that 'sensory input from outside our attention tunnels' is often missed; we simply don't notice it, as it falls outside of the laser beam, while sensory information that's within these 'tunnels' is amplified considerably for obvious reasons: all of our attention is trained on them, like a hundred microphones pointing at a buzzing bee deafening a listener. I'm a particular fan of the 'attention tunnel' analogy, as it fits so neatly with my own experience. When I'm completely engrossed in a topic of particular interest, let's say reading about it online, then I'm fixated to an uncommon degree upon the computer or the phone in my hand. In a scene reminiscent of slapstick comedy, there could be people fighting in the room with me, fires in neighbouring buildings and Godzilla crashing through the ceiling, and I believe it's likely I would not look up from my reading. At the very least, I've managed to completely miss phone calls, knocks at the door and my own body demanding that I eat or drink something *immediately*, all for the simple fact that they fall outside of this 'attention tunnel' and therefore don't really exist to me.

The possibilities behind monotropism, as an idea, are very encouraging. Although we're some way away from it being accepted generally as a central tenet of autism, I believe that it will only be a matter of time before it's recognised as such. With it may come a realigning of attitudes around what autism really means, both for individuals and for society at large. As Fergus concluded in our talk, 'We need to take seriously the advantages of monotropic hyperfocus, though. An autistic person given the time and tools they need to pursue their passions can truly be a force to be reckoned with!'

And I can't say that I disagree. I feel that given a wholesome, supportive environment, the laser focus that monotropism lends to autistic people could be a source of enormous good – not just for us, but for society at large.

BURNOUT

I hesitate to even begin this section. I've always found autistic burnout difficult to talk about, whether when speaking publicly, or when writing my blogs or my threads on Twitter. This is because it's indelibly linked in my mind to my experience of severe depression and, at times, especially around 2016 or so, attempted suicide. This is not to add a layer of hyperbole to an already difficult concept; it's simply to show how autistic burnout can leave an autistic person feeling broken, potentially forever.

All of this is made even more complicated by the fact that autistic burnout is *still* relatively unexplored and unresearched. Things are improving, but like almost everything in medicine, it takes considerable time for new ideas and medical science to trickle down to the frontline of general practitioners and nurses. As such, if (or when) an autistic person goes to their first port of call for medical assistance, they're still likely to be met with blank looks, poor-quality assumptions and a total lack of support. Any autistic person who has experienced burnout, though, can confirm that it's absolutely real. And it can be deadly.

A lot is made of statistics that show that autistic people have a much lower life expectancy than their neurotypical brethren. Depending on which set of stats you pay attention to, the life expectancy of autistic people balances out at either around thirty-six years old, or a little later at fifty-four. Both of these figures take into account many variables, from accidents to deaths caused by what we could call comorbid conditions. Of course, this does not mean that any autistic person you know will definitely be dead by their mid-fifties. Rather it's a signal of alarm that autistic people are dying much younger than they should – an alarm that really needs to be heard and reacted to. There are a whole host of factors that can drag down an autistic lifespan, many of which I've covered elsewhere in this book, but probably the most insidious (as well as potentially the most preventable) is suicide.

As I've already mentioned, autistic people are three times more likely to die as a result of suicide than the general population. Studies have shown that over 60 per cent of autistic people have at some point seriously contemplated taking their own life.*

Given the myriad struggles we face, many of which I've tried to explain in these pages, these statistics – while extraordinary – shouldn't be shocking. There's next to zero support available for the vast majority of autistic adults. Despite depression and suicidal ideation being a big part of the reason why I received a diagnosis of autism back in 2017, I've been given no support from the NHS since my diagnosis, having been sent on my way with a handful of mediocre pamphlets and a 'good luck' from the psychiatrist. We're left to try to figure it all out on our own, and if it hadn't been for the supportive network of autistic people online I fear my own personal outcome may have been bleaker.

* S. Cassidy et al., 'Risk markers for suicidality in autistic adults', *Molecular Autism*, 9(42), 31 July 2018.

And burnout so often lies as a root cause for much of this.

Autistic burnout is very much what you would expect it to be. As far as we can tell, it appears to be the eventual result of all the masking we have to do in order to fit in. As I've already mentioned, masking requires huge amounts of energy that, if I'm being brutally honest, would be put to better use keeping ourselves happy rather than keeping the neurotypical people around us happy. But it isn't. Instead, it's poured into the great act – the grand masquerade, if you like – of autistic people pretending, by any means possible, that we're just like you. And high energy usage comes at a dreadful price. Depending on the individual and, I suppose, the intensity of the masking (among other factors), autistic burnout can hit at any time. A quick headcount on Twitter suggested that an autistic person's twenties is when the risk is highest, which makes a lot of sense: school is often a place where masking is intolerably intensive (as you'll see in Chapter 5), and so having to continue this into the workforce is likely to push a person beyond their capacity. I was lucky, in a sense, that it didn't happen to me until I was thirty-three.

My burnout is obviously unique to me, and I cannot say that it's some kind of 'gold standard' to base all understanding of the phenomenon on, but I think it holds up as a reasonable example of how it works and what the effects are on a person's life, so I'll try to explain it. I had masked very successfully for at least two decades by this point – successfully enough that neither I, nor anyone I knew, had ever raised the possibility of my being autistic. Without knowing it, I'd been rerouting a considerable amount of energy and brainpower on this act for a very long time. The dam burst after the birth of my daughter, as the sudden huge change in routine, heightened responsibility and lack of downtime contributed (along with an increasingly high-pressure job) to a sharp and terrifying collapse in my ability to function. In layman's terms I guess it would be labelled a 'breakdown', but I feel that term is too generalised to be of much use.

I suddenly began to fall apart at work. I was a teacher, and pretty well regarded despite my comical lack of organisation, and I was seen as excellent at working with disenfranchised students. But over a period of maybe six months my ability to handle the strains of work unravelled, I was getting migraines very frequently and was taking too much time off work. Colleagues at work were noticing, which made it even worse, and I was forgetting hugely important things – I recall getting an email one Friday morning from the headteacher, asking for a 'chat' (is there *anything* more alarming than that?), and in the meeting being told I was in considerable trouble for not attending the training session the night before, as I mentioned in Chapter 3. I'd completely forgotten – my brain simply wasn't working properly – and after I left his office I broke down in tears. I ended up taking a long period of sick leave and my standing at work never recovered. I can directly trace my no longer being a teacher back to that moment.

I was very depressed, totally unable to fix my mask and had lost interest in all of my special interests. LEGO,

Minecraft, and football and video games generally ceased to bring any comfort, and even the miraculous success of my football club – Leicester City – in winning the Premier League in 2016 brought me little joy, comparative to how I'd have felt a few years before about such an achievement. Burnout robbed me of the enjoyment of the first years of my daughter's life, and even now, six years on, I'm not properly recovered. I still have bouts of intense depression and moments where I feel like my mask never got properly fixed. The Covid pandemic hasn't helped, of course, and I continue to shield and still don't get any practice at socialising. I often wonder what I'll be like when I can finally rejoin the rest of the world – I fear that my ability to mask in social situations will have evaporated, like drizzle on the wind.

Autistic burnout is like a severe bout of depression in many ways. The lethargy is there, as is the loss of interest in the things in life. Low mood and damaged relationships also occur, but there are differences. The most obvious difference is the fact that burnout has a definite material effect on our ability to do one particular thing – namely masking. The loss of ability to mask appears to be, for some at least, permanent. This is one of the things that makes it so damaging. As an autistic person's ability to mask is often so fundamental in their ability to manage life, and especially work, a sudden inability to do it has the potential to rip a life apart. This is the ironic and, let's face it, pretty awful truth behind masking. It causes us harm, and by rights we shouldn't have to do it, but with the way the world is currently set up we simply have to mask. In doing so, however, we literally destroy our ability to do so. We may then lose our job, we may lose our family.

Some in the community may lose their life. Consider how a person in authority, capable of violence, may regard an autistic person incapable of masking. Every year there are reports of Black autistics being injured or killed by police due to displaying ordinary autistic traits when under stress. This happened, for example, to Linden Cameron in Salt Lake City, Utah. After his mother had contacted police, wanting help to get him treatment, he was shot repeatedly and seriously injured. Demands that he lie on the ground had been ignored, and as a result he was almost killed.

I'd imagine any autistic person reading this would recognise a feeling of being unable to comply with such an order if in a heightened state of stress or meltdown, and especially if a generalised fear of the police was present. An inability to mask in a situation like this, when any behaviour deemed as 'non-standard' could combine with belonging to an already persecuted minority to lead to outcomes like this, could be fatal. It's vital for people in authority to understand the limitations of autistic masking, and to be able to recognise the signs of autistic meltdown and autistic behaviour generally. Realistically, for this to happen, we'd need to see new mandatory training for the police, rather like that delivered to NHS workers, so that mistakes of this nature were minimised. At present that feels a long way off, although good work is done by the National Police Autism Association in raising awareness. However, it goes without saying that if burnout contributes to an inability to mask oneself out of a terrifying situation like this, then the added danger is palpable.

As I've said, it was becoming a father that sparked this conflagration of masking ability. I truly believe that one of the causes was being unable to indulge in my special interests due to the new pressure of looking after a tiny human. I had used video games and guitar playing in particular as emotional cleansers and rechargers, bringing me back up to an even keel when I was in danger of capsizing spectacularly, and having no time or space to do these things anymore hit me very hard indeed. I'm not saying that losing the ability to have fun with my favourite interests was the sole cause, but I fervently believe that it was a huge part of it. The danger for an autistic person losing access to those things they enjoy doing most is very real and potentially life threatening, in my opinion, something well worth considering when you threaten to ban an autistic person from playing their favourite video game because they embarrassed you with a meltdown in public.

It often feels like burnout is essentially inevitable for autistic people. Indeed, when I asked my part of the community about it, I got hundreds of responses outlining when burnout hit them for the first time, with most respondents making it clear that it was a repeated experience for them, rather than a grim one-off. I suppose the fact the world is really not well set up for us is the biggest problem. We're always, it feels, on the margins, struggling to fit ourselves into a society that knows nothing about how we work or why we struggle; not only that, but said society is overtly hostile to us, due to our inherent difference, forcing us to hide ourselves and cease displaying our true behaviours. Throw on top of this all of the stress from miscommunication and sensory sensitivity, and we have a perfect storm of factors that will bring down any autistic person.

So how can we change things for the better? Well, all of the advice I've tried to give elsewhere in this book will help, of course. But if we're to focus specifically on special interests, then there are a few ways that burnout might be mitigated, if not completely avoided:

- Never curtail an autistic person's access to their interests. Do not view these interests as merely hobbies, nor the autistic person as 'entitled' or 'bratty' (two terms I've seen used by *teachers*) for wanting to be able to indulge in them. You must understand the regulatory benefits they have, and the way they enable us autistic people to manage our stress levels so we're able to get on with our day.

- Gently encourage autistic people close to you (in terms of society, not proximity – don't go around bothering autistic strangers) to indulge in their interests when they're struggling. I often forget about them when I need them most, though that might be more to do with being ADHD than anything else.

- Take an interest, or at the very least *feign* an interest, in our favourite stuff. It goes such a long way to making me feel accepted when I get the chance to talk about my interests. This is particularly powerful with autistic children, who will often talk about their interests anyway, whether you're listening or not. Just sometimes, actually tune in and participate.

As I said, this is not enough to completely prevent burn-out. If we're to have any hope of reducing it in autistic people, then there needs to be a widespread effort of genuine acceptance covering all aspects of life, but in terms of special interests these things will help.

5

SCHOOL: THE HARSHEST ENVIRONMENT

NOT DESIGNED FOR US

Of course, there's one thing about life as a child that's almost guaranteed to hobble our opportunities to enjoy our interests, unless we're exceptionally lucky: school. Time spent in the school is time dragged away from the things that keep us balanced. But that's the least of our worries in the recurring nightmare that is the classroom.

Schools have been around for a long time. The idea of gathering up large numbers of children and placing them in a single location to be taught by those capable of sharing their knowledge is no new thing, being probably almost as old as civilisation itself. There's plentiful evidence that the civilisations that sprouted in Sumeria and Babylon in the Fertile Crescent had established school settings where children were taught language skills and history (presumably quite quickly).

But from that time onwards, schools have been designed with aims and ambitions in mind that are not well suited to the neurodivergent minority. After all, autism wasn't described until the early years of the twentieth century and our understanding of it even in the 2020s is far from complete. Generation after generation of autistic children have been taught in establishments that gave absolutely no conscious thought to being accommodating for those with a different type of brain and a different perception of the world. By the time I entered education in the late 1980s, schools were about as well adapted for my neurotype as a set of stairs is adapted for the use by a Dalek.

Room layout and the structure of school buildings are one of the bigger reasons why neurodivergent children struggle in school, and certainly the most intractable. After all, it isn't easy to knock down a flawed design and build a brand new one, and anyway there's no real consensus as to what a good autistic-friendly school would even look like, though I have some ideas. There are the issues of narrow corridors, limited ways in and out of buildings, the ever-present strip lighting, and a lack of places for quiet, introverted students to hide themselves away at lunchtime. On top of that, there's the strange phenomenon of open-plan classrooms.

My first school that I can remember clearly was a typical modern school, built in the 1960s, all glass and wooden inserts and partitions. It was an open-plan building, far removed from the tight little classrooms favoured by the builders of the older Victorian schools that dot the country. Light, and filled with air and colour, I'm sure that many of the people in the place thought it was delightful.

I hated it.

Much like the issues with open-plan offices I'll mention later in the book, the stubborn refusal to partition things with proper walls meant that every inch of the main building was a cacophony of horror to my sensitive little ears. When I was sitting reading in one 'classroom', I could hear everything happening over in the Year 3 area, as it was separated from me by nothing more than low bookcases, pot plants and delusion. Every cry, laugh, grunt and exasperated teacher's voice carried across the whole space, and I remember finding it incredibly hard to concentrate on anything at all. When my teacher was talking, explaining to us whatever activity we were about to be unleashed upon, I'd have to strain to differentiate their voice from the general din surrounding me. It's incredibly difficult to do this as an autistic person. I suppose neurotypical people have some kind of built-in filter that enables them to tune in to whatever is the most important sound in the vicinity, but I'm afraid I don't have that feature.

As far as my brain is concerned, all sounds are of equal importance and it will strain to catch the details in every single utterance that crams itself into my ears. Even now, sitting in a coffee shop can be a trial of patience as I try to focus on whatever I'm meant to be doing, while the hissing and burping of the coffee machines and the various conversations held by staff and patrons push their way into my brain uninvited. As an adult I've developed strategies for managing this, mostly involving listening to music on headphones (this seems to feed the monotropic within me, as my attention is sucked into the tune and everything else fades), but as a kid I didn't have the wherewithal to do this – I could barely brush my teeth without incident – so I just accepted that sounds were a strange and energy-sapping part of life.

Happily, my time at that school was reasonably short, and by the time I was eight years old I'd been moved to a much older school – one of those brick Victorian affairs – and settled into learning in proper classrooms delineated by cold, hard bricks and paint. Every teacher had their own actual room, and the difference was incredible. In a school like this, when the room is filled with silent kids engrossed in their reading, then it's actually quiet. Apart from the occasional crash of a door somewhere far off in the depths of all that brickwork, or the muffled shout of a teacher as they attempt to stop a student drawing a portrait of their best friend on their best friend's face, all is peaceful and serene.

When we come to secondary schools, the problem of narrow corridors causes problems for neurodivergent students. Because tradition dictates that all lessons begin and end as one, every fifty minutes or so the corridors suddenly become awash with children, all crushed in, elbowing their way from place to place. For an autistic student with sensitivity to sound, smell and touch, these regular ruckuses are horrifying. The constant unwanted touches as knees and feet and bags hoisted onto shoulders buffet to and fro is enough to fast-track any autistic person to meltdown, and even as a teacher in adulthood I found my stress levels peaking when caught in the rush.

Considering I'm a bulky 6 foot 7 tall and still found it rough, imagine what it must be like for a little Year 7 student trying to get from Maths to Music and surrounded by jostling sixteen-year-olds.

These same awful crowds occur at external doors too, as students are desperate for the open air to enjoy their downtime, and appear around the lunch queue too. It's quite commonplace for students who cannot move around as easily for whatever reason to get a pass to allow them to leave lessons five minutes early so they can avoid this nightmare. I strongly recommend that this courtesy also be extended to autistic students as a matter of course.

It's safe to assume that a large number of autistic children will struggle to use the lunch hour for its main purpose of eating, having been defeated by the crowds around the food queue, and will probably enter the afternoon's lessons hungry and distracted. However, what of the breaktime's secondary purpose – enjoying a bit of a rest from all that learning? Well, things go wrong here too.

We have breaktime in school and in the workplace to give people a breather, a moment to recuperate from the hard work they do in their classrooms and workplaces. Their whole point in schools is to enable children to decompress for a few minutes, mess about, socialise, use up some of that energy. The idea is that after running around screaming for twenty minutes, kids are then ready for their next chunk of learning. And for the most part it works like that. Children who wish to socialise get a chance to do so. Children who'd prefer to dash about and kick a ball at other children are likewise catered for.

But it doesn't work so well for some autistic children. Many autistic students, as with the general autistic population, live their lives in a permanent state of extreme stress. As I've explained, this is a major reason why autistic meltdowns happen more frequently than neurotypical meltdowns. We're all closer to our ceiling of tolerance. So if a student is stressed in class (and the next section will explain how this is pretty much a given), then their need for a restful breaktime is absolutely paramount, and it would be a disaster should that breaktime not offer the requisite relaxation.

And it so rarely does. Once again, the physical architecture of the school building and the timing and structure of the school day simply don't offer what autistic children so frequently need: a place and time to decompress and relax on their own terms. Sure, some autistic kids will relish going out and expending energy with their friends, but many would rather go somewhere dark, cool and quiet where they can be completely alone and unbothered by teachers, peers or even friends. Does such a place exist in a school? Well, informally, yes – of course. Every school will have areas hidden beneath staircases, or little cupboards filled with books, or offices that are rarely, if ever, used. It's just that children typically are not allowed to be in these spaces. Teachers 'on duty' are tasked with rooting them out and ushering them outdoors into the glare of the sunshine and their curious classmates. If any kid is found in such a quiet, peaceful spot then the natural assumption is that they're up to something nefarious and need to be reprimanded before it's too late.

It's important to accept that this is a form of discrimination that's as damaging as it is easy to correct. Autistic children who want to hide away somewhere quiet and chill out soon learn that such a sensible act of self-care is somehow forbidden, a lesson they may carry around for years and years. In pushing them into busy areas filled with peers they're essentially being forced to socialise against their will, which will involve masking – and, as I hope you remember, forcing kids (or indeed any autistic person) to mask is, in its own way, an act of violence. As a direct result of all of this, huge numbers of autistic children will be trooping back into classrooms once breaktime is over even more exhausted and burned out than they were twenty minutes earlier.

And we wonder why autistic children refuse to go to school.

Making provisions for autistic kids to have a safe place where they're allowed (or even better, *encouraged*) to go is an act of genuine equity and would cost barely anything. Ideally, it would be a blanket rule change whereby any child who wanted to rest in a quiet spot would automatically be allowed to do so. This would help include all of those thousands of children who are autistic but don't have a diagnosis. Teachers could continue to roam the school to make sure nothing bad happens, but without that attitude of 'all children are up to no good' that seems to permeate all too often. However, as a realist who knows how education systems work, a more immediately palatable move would be, at the very least, to allow those students who have a diagnosis to make use of these quiet zones without being treated as deviants.

Allowing autistic children to avoid the intense crowds of school life in these various ways is a basic provision that should be available everywhere. They require little in the way of management or funding, but can reduce the stresses of the school day. As is always the case, the barrier to this is simple knowledge and understanding – being aware of the problem in the first place. Well, as you're here reading this, now you know. If you work in education, spread the word. If you're a parent, ask the school for adjustments. However, the problems of school are not limited to the building as a whole, nor the travails of the school day. The classrooms themselves represent a gigantic barrier for many autistic students.

CLASSROOM PERILS

I think it's a very safe bet that you'll be able to remember some of the classrooms you inhabited in your school years. I'd wager even further that if you could get just the briefest whiff of the smell of a school science lab you'd be transported back to chemistry lessons in an instant. These places stay with you, and for many these memories are relatively happy, possibly even cosy. But perhaps not for all of us.

As a teacher, I had very little need to ever visit the science or technology departments; I was basically a hermit in my own classroom, after all. But on those few times I did walk to the other end of the building I was always struck by a familiar olfactory jolt. Both departments had such a recognisable smell – technology had a strong whiff of sawdust and glue, while science had a smell I've never identified. It just *is*, in science rooms in schools all over the country. Perhaps it's a mingling of gas from the gas taps, burned gauzes and chemicals, or perhaps it's the science teachers themselves – who knows. Yet every time I went near these classrooms I was transported back to some of the most traumatic times in my childhood – being in lessons where I was terrified all of the time.

I'm an English graduate, and have been more comfortable passively sitting and reading or writing all my life. As far as I'm concerned, all the best things involve sitting down quietly in some way, where the most physical movement required is the lifting of a coffee cup or the twirling of thumbs over a video game controller. The word 'practical' makes me feel very uneasy, and the notion of anything being 'physical' brings me out in a cold sweat. As such, I was not an enormous fan of practical or physical education lessons in school.

Ninety per cent of my time in school was spent sitting at a desk with a pen and pencil, a bit of paper or an exercise book, with ample opportunity to daydream or doodle as a means of keeping my stress levels – always as high as they could go without me breaking down completely – nice and steady. I enjoyed this bit of school. The predictability of every lesson having a similar structure, the tranquillity of reading a text, the calm and joy of writing a story about zombies attacking me in a cave filled with pirates.

But always lurking, just out of sight, were the twin horrors of science or woodwork practicals and PE. By 'science practical', I mean those lessons where the desks were cleared and the apparatus of scientific endeavour was laid out carefully – Bunsen burners, flasks, wires, fuses, bits of dead frog – you know the kind of thing. Most children in my class absolutely loved this shit – the opportunity to mess around with electricity or, even better, actual *fire* was a fantastic break in their lives, and they responded to it with gusto. Meanwhile, I was sitting there, gazing around in horror at all of this awful *practicality*, terrified that something dreadful was going to happen, stressed beyond reason by the uprooting of the routine I was so in love with.

It was always the same – the other students would be clattering around with their equipment, always inexplicably busy and focused on what they were doing, while I had absolutely no idea. I didn't know why I didn't know what was going on. I always listened to the teacher diligently and carefully wrote down the instructions, and I understood them too. But for some reason I just couldn't follow them. My mind spent most of its processing power on second guessing potential mistakes and mishaps, to the point where the original simple running order of steps was lost in the mire.

Typically, I'd find myself sitting there, staring nonplussed at the bendy rubber tube of a Bunsen burner in one hand and a test tube in the other, desperately trying to work out what the hell I was meant to be doing with these two meaningless objects. I was petrified that in my ignorance I would incinerate the whole classroom or shatter the flasks that we had been told were *so* expensive, and in this ignorance I essentially paralysed myself. Time after time, these science practicals ended, for me, in bitter disappointment. Everyone else made funky multicoloured flames or clocks that ran on the electrical energy of a tangerine while I sat there quietly sobbing with frustration, a piece of litmus paper stuck to my fingers.

I now know that my inability to follow the kind of verbal instructions that featured so heavily in these lessons was down to my being neurodivergent. It seems to be mostly an ADHD thing, though there are lots of features of autism at play too. And it has never gone away. All you would have to do to see a modern iteration of the phenomenon would be to watch me trying to follow a yoga video on YouTube. The fast-paced instructions involving body parts, left and right, and various shapes and positions leave me in a completely bewildered knot on the floor. Of course, back in the 1990s, in a small middle school in Leicestershire, nobody knew that my neurotype was the cause of my bewilderment, and most science teachers wrote me off as a failure before I had much chance.

Of course, I was a good enough masker that I wouldn't betray much of this inner turmoil to my classmates or teacher. Instead, it was all swallowed, like a slow-working poison, as I attempted to fit in with the giddy joy of my friends when the liquid in the test-tube began turning blue. Fake smile affixed, I would expend so much energy trying to avoid embarrassing myself by having a meltdown that the important part of the experiment – the learning – was completely missed. I don't think I learned anything from these practicals, other than perfecting my mask and my breath control. Everything I now know about the various processes we were meant to be exploring I've since learned from my random adventures in Wikipedia.

Now, I know that this is certainly not a universal trait – plenty of autistic people will have enjoyed the practical aspects of lessons like these and may well have made a career out of them. But I offer it as an example of the kind of routine-breaking stress that can occur frequently at school. Clearly, for my autistic brain, the shift from the calm of book-work to the noise and smells of practical activity was far too much to handle, and my learning suffered as a result.

This is what needs to be forever at the front of teachers' minds when they set up their lessons: how autistic students react to the various 'flavours' of lessons that they offer, and how some formats will be so difficult for some students that they might as well not be in the classroom, given how little they'll learn or understand as a result. Tailoring autistic students' education more explicitly and carefully is an interesting thought experiment, but one that's often simply thrown out for being untenable. Yet if a particular type of classroom activity (or indeed work-based activity – it's still a relevant concern after the age of eighteen) causes a great deal of harm for very little payback, then what *is* the point in insisting on it?

Perhaps, rather than insisting that autistic students somehow deal with this stress, it might be possible to allow them to simply *observe* the activity as it occurs – either a group of other students doing the experiment or the teacher leading from the front? That's certainly what I always dreamed of, and I was ecstatic the few times it happened, as my attention could be focused on the processes that were taking place, without being distracted by anxiety.

When I was training to be a teacher, back in around 2008 or so, an absolutely sacrosanct part of our teaching practice was getting the students to work together in groups. It was seen as a fundamental part of learning, a vital ingredient in every lesson plan. If you tried to teach a lesson without it then your mentor would mark you down, lamenting the missed opportunities that now would seriously affect the students' ability to learn.

Trouble was, I absolutely *hated* group work back at school. Every single time it was forced upon me – especially in those awful science practical lessons, but also in English, maths and geography – I'd find myself mentally curling into a ball and clamming up completely, hoping that the ordeal would soon be over. As a result I found it very difficult to enforce such things on the students in my care. However, if I was to get my teaching degree I had to toe the line and do as I was told, so I gradually became a teacher who tried to incorporate group work into as many lessons as I could.

Now, I don't want to start casting aspersions on others' teaching practice, nor do I wish to make the claim that group work is universally bad. I'm sure that it suits many students very nicely. Perhaps there are even some autistic people who enjoy working in groups around a classroom table – we're such a varied bunch that I'd not be surprised. However, I feel it's safe to say that group work is not something that many autistic adults look back on fondly. I put a call out on Twitter, asking for thoughts on group work and science experiments, just to get a feel for where we stand, and the response was overwhelming. The hatred of group work, after all these years! Reply after reply outlined the horrors of being forced to work with peers and the damage it did to the learning experience. I'd been expecting a decent response, but this was something else entirely. One person summed my experience up perfectly, saying that 'it seemed a burdensome hassle', that it quickly led to their being overwhelmed and that groups were a 'big negative'. Similar responses abounded.

Clearly, autism and group work in schools do not mix.

To understand why, we have to rewind back to the early chapters of this book, and the issues around communication and socialising. If you recall, one problem that almost all autistic people have is a history of trauma based on failed communication – misunderstandings, jokes that didn't work, misinterpretation of motives, that sort of thing. After years of this, we understandably wish to reduce the opportunities for such missteps; we begin to become more introverted, more closeted, and keep ourselves safe and alone as much as possible. An autistic school child, around their early teens, will almost certainly have learned this already. Thus, forcing them to team up with other people, re-opening these wounds and making them vulnerable to the unpleasant possibility of further communication crises is a bit of a – if you'll excuse the vernacular – dick move. It gets much worse if the autistic child is in some other way part of an intersecting minority. If, for example, they're also trans or non-binary, or if they're from a minority ethnic background, then the chance of a negative social outcome rockets up thanks to the various prejudices that are still alive and kicking in the 2020s.

Group work takes a safe and solitary activity – that of working quietly on one's own work in the organised space of the classroom – and turns it on its head. The teacher, who'd ordinarily be able to monitor for social unpleasantness with reasonable ease, is now less able to intervene. Each group becomes its own little kingdom, with leaders and followers quickly establishing themselves, and with autistic children caught up in these petty politics. Given that these kinds of political games are very challenging for most autistic students, this will regularly lead to unpleasantness. Leaders are seldom appointed – instead they occur organically, as the most extrovert and confident child begins to grasp control of the whole endeavour, while the others in the group are reduced to seething jealousy or a complete misunderstanding of the developing power dynamic.

As the leader exerts their new, dizzying power, an autistic member of the group may misjudge things –

perhaps talk too much about what they want to do or encroach unknowingly on the leader's turf, meting out roles and tasks in a way that seems logical. Suddenly, without any warning, the leader is furious and puts the autistic student in their place, perhaps by ignoring them, perhaps by insulting or mocking them, perhaps by a sophisticated melding of the two.

The trouble is, autistic people usually find it difficult enough to negotiate through ordinary social interactions with peers, so the moment that power dynamics are thrown into the mix things can get confusing quickly. I remember learning early on in school that it didn't matter how good your ideas were: sometimes people simply didn't want to hear them. Even now, approaching forty, this fact blows my mind a little – how much genius have we discounted as a species due to this foolish trait? – and I still cannot reconcile myself to it. Unless you're in the 'it crowd' or the 'in group' or with the 'fashionable people', your opinion is, apparently, inherently trash. I'd sit during group work as a child, knowing the answers, knowing what needed to be done, but because I was the slightly odd, quiet kid, my input was unwelcome and generally ignored. And I do mean ignored – as in, I'd speak and everyone would glaze over slightly, wait for me to finish (if I was lucky) and then continue wondering together what the solution was. Autism is called an 'invisible disability', and sometimes I think that term might be more literal than we realise.

Even if the autistic kid has some kind of social cachet and is therefore not simply ignored, the struggle to be heard can be very tough. The usual problems of not knowing when to speak, not understanding when a person has finished their utterance, not being able to moderate the volume of our impassioned and excited voices – these all conspire against us, pushing us to the periphery of the group, and making our contribution lesser and lesser.

As a result of all of this, in my later years of teaching – particularly after my diagnosis – I moved away from group work unless it was absolutely necessary. Witnessing the age-old misery of a child wandering around the classroom looking plaintively for a group that would accept them became a thing of the past. I'd do all I could to reduce the level of social isolation students faced, knowing all too well how corrosive it was to young souls. If, however, it's absolutely necessary to make autistic people work in groups at times, then I'd recommend the following:

- Appoint leaders and other roles very clearly before the group begins their work – that way nothing is left to ambiguity.
- Allow autistic students to be additions to otherwise full or complete groups; likewise, allow autistic students to form smaller groups than you'd otherwise prefer: either of these allows flexibility for autistic people who'd rather be a face in the crowd or be in a more close-knit group. Basically, don't be too rigid in your expectation of group size.
- Keep an eye on groups with autistic students – not to be punitive, but simply to monitor the

interactions and ensure that things don't dissolve into bullying. You want to ensure that they feel safe and supported, and not abandoned.

WHY ARE WE LABELLED 'CHALLENGING?'

Every Friday from 1997 through to 1999 I'd sit on my sofa at home, a sixteen-year-old with my school bag limply in my hand, trying to pluck up the courage to get up, go out of the front door and walk the hundred yards or so to my school. I would sit for up to fifteen minutes, paralysed by a cascading crash of unbidden thoughts and worries about the day to come. If I managed to succeed, I'd usually find myself getting into school late, having to sign the late book and getting a glare from my form tutor. If I was unsuccessful, and it did occasionally happen, my mum would find me still on the sofa after dropping my little sister off at primary school, long after the school day had begun without me.

The main worry I was facing was PE. Physical Education had always been a serious problem for me. The stress of having to get changed in a room full of loud, obnoxious boys was too much for my senses, and I hated the break in my routine. I also hated sports. I not only hated the physicality of them, as I have little coordination, but also the way we were meant to somehow understand the rules without ever having them explained to us. I'm not diagnosed with dyspraxia, nor have I pursued a diagnosis, but I know from listening to dyspraxic autistic people that finding the physical requirements of sports and games difficult is a common problem. How far autistic people without a discrete diagnosis of dyspraxia struggle with physicality is a little less clear, but a hatred of PE lessons within the community is a shared experience.

I vividly remember being forced into playing football, with the teacher joining the opposing team – one of the maths teachers, an imposing fellow with little regard for 'namby pambies' like me who could barely kick a ball. In scenes so reminiscent of *Kes* that I'd respect your scepticism in accepting that this actually happened, I found myself continually berated for my lack of skill by a grown man who clearly thought he was one of Manchester United's greatest missed opportunities. Being very tall, it was assumed by all of the other players that I'd be a monster in the air, heading balls into the net with abandon like an East Midlands Cristiano Ronaldo but with bad acne. Instead, all that transpired was a number of boys kicking heavy footballs at my head from every direction as I tried to duck and dive out of the way. I think I managed to successfully head the ball only once, and that was by accident – you see, my dodging skills are just as flawed as the rest – and I helplessly watched it sail into my own team's goal.

In short, I was poorly adapted to this and found the experience so humiliating that it precipitated a terror of going into school on days when I'd be expected to endure this nonsense. I'd do everything I could to avoid having to go out on that field in my PE kit. Normally a quiet, well-behaved kid, I resorted to lying through my teeth to PE teachers week after week – I'd forgotten my kit, or I had the flu, or I had a tummy ache, or I'd broken my hip – whatever the excuse, I'd find myself in the library or on the viewing balcony above the sports hall, happily reading my book while my classmates smashed into each other and showed off their physical skills. Because of how poorly the school was accommodating my particular neurodivergence, I was forced to rebel and lie and dissemble, despite the fact that doing so went against every law-abiding, if clumsy, bone in my body. Why couldn't they allow me to play sports that weren't team games – like badminton or tennis – or ones that were more ordered and structured, like athletics? Why was it always *football and rugby*, for goodness's sake?

This is the conundrum that education poses to autistic students. Many will have little desire to kick up a fuss and certainly none whatsoever to get into trouble (after all, sticking to the rules and avoiding 'rocking the boat' are key traits shared by many autistic people), but they'll have absolutely no choice when push comes to shove. In my case the stakes were low and I only had to resort to telling fibs about my PE kit or having a bad cold, but for some autistic children things can rapidly become very serious, and all because there was no accommodation made towards them in the first place.

The most obvious situation of this ilk that's seen across the country, if not the world, is school absenteeism. The idea of 'school refusal', where a child refuses so steadfastly to go into school that parents and teachers can end up out of options, was alien to me when I first started teaching (mostly because it had never occurred to me as a student myself that this was a possibility), but I quickly noticed how prevalent it was, especially as students got older.

The problem is compounded by the fact that accommodation in lessons is so rare. Certainly, back in the 1990s, teachers had no patience at all for students who, for example, couldn't catch. The inability to do these kinds of apparently 'easy' tasks was seen as a result of laziness, or an unacceptable flaw that had to be corrected or, worse, mocked. Students who genuinely couldn't throw, or kick, or catch, or indeed write for prolonged periods or focus on their work, were seen as immediate failures and even laughing stocks. On top of this, classrooms were sensory nightmares, with brash strip lighting, colourful posters covering every inch of wall and strong air fresheners or the teachers' aftershave or perfume filling our nostrils. None of this engendered a love of school in us.

A natural result of this constant fighting against hostility is resistance. Sometimes this will be relatively passive, like the school refusal I referred to earlier, or a student like myself hiding towards the back of the class and avoiding any kind of interaction with peers or staff. However, it can equally lead to a more active resistance that might manifest in what is often described as 'challenging' behaviour. Now, this topic alone could fill a million books, and I won't attempt to cover the huge complexities at work here. All I seek to do is open your eyes to why an autistic child might resort to behaviour that could be seen as 'bad'.

Imagine a school child who is struggling to cope with the sensory input in the classroom. They're tired and stressed, as every noise is smashing into their ears like crowds struggling to get onto a train on the Underground. They've already experienced various social issues today (and it's only 10 a.m.), having not understood a sarcastic comment made by a friend earlier. They feel alone and confused, as if the world is out to get them. They're struggling to marshal their thoughts and keep on task, but it is noisy and too colourful and too smelly in the room. Suddenly the teacher challenges them because they're not writing anything, and demands that they focus and get on with their work.

Unless you yourself are autistic, have ADHD or are in some other way neurodivergent, it will be very difficult for you to understand the levels of stress we're talking about here. They're not the same levels of stress you might feel in this situation. Instead, imagine you've just been delivered a gas bill that's too enormous to afford, you've just been demoted at work, your spouse or best friend is starting a fight with you and you've got a really bad headache.

Now ... how would you react to an officious teacher telling you to get on with your work?

It may feel like I've utilised some hyperbole here in the comparison, but you'd be surprised by how unexaggerated this is. After all, children generally tend to view daily challenges as the be-all and end-all, so it would make sense that an autistic child will be similar. Though being demoted at work and dealing with childhood social stress may feel to you to be worlds apart, my gentle advice would be not to be so confident in this. As I've said before, many times, the general level of stress that autistic people run at is much, much higher than that of non-autistic people; an autistic child in a classroom may very well be feeling as much stress as you would associate with much bigger problems. And so the fightback against the teacher, whether it be a simple refusal or something rather more 'colourful', though not a good thing in itself, should at least be more understandable.

But it isn't. Instead, too many autistic children (who may be reacting to intolerable levels of stress that they struggle to articulate) are written off as challenging, naughty, difficult and worse. Many of them will experience being excluded repeatedly, as their behaviour never improves. And why would it if their stressors remain the same? Unless work is undertaken to actually remove the causes of stress for these children, then how is it reasonable to expect them to become better at managing them, especially if they have no support? Too often this cycle is repeated to the point of permanent exclusion, at which moment their lives will be irreparably damaged.

I don't wish to excuse bad behaviour that's simply bad behaviour. This can exist, though it's almost always worth considering if there's a need being communicated in some way. Sometimes the 'kickback' against the stress can take physical form, and people can be hurt. In these cases, further assistance is obviously required for both the student and the school, as well as the parents. However, it seems ridiculous to me that we expend so much energy on expecting these children to somehow adapt to intolerable environments and never once consider altering the environments so they're adapted to the children. Surely we're looking at things the wrong way round.

Some autistic students thrive in school. Others, like me, appear to thrive, while hiding the real struggle behind a veneer of masking. Still others find it such a struggle that masking is impossible, or they're unable to mask in the first place. There is, as always, a wide variety of experience. But for those students who find school difficult or impossible, much remains to be done to help them, even in this age of 'autism awareness'. Awareness, after all, does not necessarily equal action.

What can be done? First, all teachers working with autistic students need up-to-date training on how autism works. This must be delivered, at least in part, by autistic people themselves. Myths and stereotypes still linger in schools, and what we thought was good practice even in 2010 is now hopelessly dated and often actively counter-productive. Teachers need to know exactly how autistic people tend to experience the world, in order to make the best decisions regarding how they should be taught. After all, once you know that a student is doodling because it genuinely helps them to concentrate, why would you have a problem with their page of little drawings?

Beyond this, we need to see improved cultures in schools, where autism ceases to be a 'taboo' term and where neurotypical students actually know about autism too. Making autism a natural part of school life, as natural as dyslexia has become, would go a long way to normalising autistic students' experiences and perhaps counter the 'othering' that so frequently occurs. When I was a teacher, I was open about being autistic and, over time, autistic students began to be similarly open. The other students were not fazed by this; in fact, one class of particularly 'cool' kids, who were generally pretty mean to outsiders, became fascinated by the autistic experience that I and a handful of other students could describe, and became wonderfully accepting and relaxed about our traits and behaviours – to the point where I feel we were able to unmask a little. I miss that class, and I wonder what the impact would be if this were to be replicated across the whole country.

OFF TO UNIVERSITY

I never truly intended to go to university – not with any grand idea in mind, at least. I'd no real ambition because it was (and still is) impossible for me to plan that far in advance (my limit is planning for the next five days. Beyond lie chaos and chance). As such, I ended up at university simply by default. I'd done reasonably well in my A levels, and was ushered by my school into considering different universities as my natural next-stage-of-life. No one ever asked me if I really wanted to do it; but then, I didn't ask myself either. I remember my school being very keen that I should try to get into Oxford or Cambridge. Oxford was out because I didn't like the 'colour' of the word itself – something about it made me feel uneasy (read up on synaesthesia if you want to know more). 'Cambridge' felt nicer when I said it, and as a bonus wasn't too far away. But on visiting the place I was intimidated by the extreme grandeur of the place (Downing College's dining hall made me feel sick with fear, it's so extravagant).

Going to university was going to be a huge enough upheaval in my daily routine; to make it so different from the life I knew would have been folly. I had no idea I was autistic – I didn't even know what that was at this point – and yet I made a choice that was perfect for my neurodivergent self. Rather than put myself through the strains of trying to fit in to the upper-middle-class environs of Cambridge, I would send myself back 'home' to go to university in Loughborough, where I'd spent my childhood between the ages of four and seven. The familiarity of the place was tinged with a genuine affection; I had many happy memories of the town from my years there as a little kid, from the big McDonald's in the town centre (where I'd sat quietly in the corner at many a friend's birthday party), to the yearly funfair that filled the market place, to the little streams and woods on the outskirts of town where I'd spent time looking for interesting fish and chasing ducklings. Returning there at the age of eighteen was a decision wisely taken.

I hesitated to write about university in this chapter. After all, not all autistic people will make it to university, and being able to get a degree, even before the massive ramping up of tuition fees, is a big privilege, and Lord knows I've enough of those. However, a lot of autistic people do make it through to higher education and our collective experiences of that life are not brilliantly documented, nor are they included in books about autistic people written by neurotypicals. For these reasons I feel that exploring it briefly here will certainly do no harm. As we continue to realise just how many people are autistic, I expect that this broadening out of which experiences can class as 'relevant' will continue.

Going to university is, in many ways, a gentler introduction to the adult world for some autistic people than an alternative where they may leave school and immediately join the job market. After all, the routines and schedules that made school life manageable (at times, at least) continue fairly uninterrupted, as do the expectations and the nature of the work undertaken. The school holidays persist, though get a little longer. The weekly structure of lessons on a timetable continues, as does the system of homework and deadlines. For a person like me, moving into an essay-based degree, the shift from my A levels was barely discernible. At least that was the case academically.

The reason university could be seen as being a rather rougher transition is the move from living at the family home with your parents, to living alone in some weird and wonderful student accommodation, often in a town or city that's completely alien, with little to no support from any adults nearby. For someone who has very carefully demarcated their days and weeks thanks to years of experience of living with their family in their house, the shift can be dizzying and extraordinarily stressful.

In addition, there's often very little formal support for autistic students, even now. I've heard from many autistic students, or ex-students who were at university recently, and found that although there's an increasing willingness by some universities to accommodate basic academic preferences, such as exam access changes and deadline extensions, there's still a general feeling that this isn't widespread enough, with 40 per cent of the 300-plus people I heard from saying that they received 'no accommodation' of this sort at all. One respondent said that every single piece of accommodation had to be arranged separately, again and again, rather than there being a 'blanket notice' to staff, which seems particularly unhelpful given how notoriously complex such processes can be, and how autistic people can struggle with executive function. Other respondents noted that even where accommodations were ostensibly set up, lecturers would often ignore them or complain about them. When students are vulnerable, alone and away from family, possibly for the first time, that's not encouraging.

Even though I'd chosen a university that was situated within a familiar geography, I was still blindsided by the terrifying freedom of those first months living independently. Looking back, I was in an extremely vulnerable position and I believe that if it hadn't been for the luck of making a few good friends very quickly on campus, I may have had a far worse time of it. On the one hand, the independence meant that for the first time ever I was able to live to my own routine without interference from parents. This suited me well. On the other hand, I was suddenly prone to intense peer pressure of a type I hadn't encountered in sleepy Lincolnshire.

I vividly remember going out drinking for about five nights in succession, completely against my will, with my new flatmates in halls. Such a thing was actively encouraged by the older students, who saw the arrival of 'freshers' as an excellent opportunity to bully and abuse those less experienced than them. They acted as sheriffs, roaming the halls and dragging us from our rooms, herding us into town or onto buses to Birmingham or Leicester or Nottingham, where we would be 'encouraged' to drink our own body weight in lager mixed with cider and blackcurrant – a concoction labelled a 'purple nasty' in Loughborough.

I think most new students are vulnerable at this time, but autistic students must be more so. Alcohol is an interesting topic among autistic people, and I wouldn't wish to make generalisations about it as experiences are so varied, but when we consider how alcohol is viewed as a 'social lubricant' even among the neurotypical, it stands to reason that autistic people may see it and use it as a way to manage these difficult, traumatic social experiences. This was certainly the case for me throughout my teenage years and my early twenties. Finding socialising draining and difficult, drinking beer and wine became my way of coping, and I fear that I drank far too much. The booze may well have provided me with a coat of liquid armour against misunderstanding and crisis, and also may have boosted my confidence, allowing me to chat at length about things that weren't my special interests, but it also made me sick and wrecked the following days. The positives rarely outweighed the negatives, and as a result I rarely drink these days.

But back in 2001 we were actively encouraged to get absolutely ruined by our experienced, smirking elders.

As a 6 foot 7 white cis male, my vulnerabilities were perhaps more limited (although I distinctly remember almost getting mugged in Birmingham city centre when I ducked out of the awful 'beer hall' party I'd been dragged to). But if we consider autistic women, or people of colour, then the risks may increase depending on the kind of events they're taken to. As I mentioned, I found myself in a dangerous situation in the West Midlands because I'd left the sanctuary and safety of my group – this is generally ill advised for anyone in big scary urban areas, but what type of person is most likely to need to run away from the safety of their friendship group when things get too loud or intense? Exactly.

My autistic self, bolting into the fresh air to escape sensory and social overload only to be threatened with a knife outside is peak irony, a danger that I think more people should be aware of if they're going to insist on forcing autistic people to socialise. Alternatively, of course, perhaps there could be a change in what's expected of new students, a realisation that some may be autistic or disabled, and that forcing them to drink in strange cities might not be necessary.

I'm lucky that my experience with alcohol ended fairly benignly, with a gradual escape from its grasp as I moved through my twenties. However, I can see that my continuing social discomfort and anxiety around social events could well have led to much bleaker outcomes, and it's not as if I can now socialise without using alcohol as a support; far from it – my lack of interest in and tolerance for drinking these days is matched by an absolute lack of socialising. As I can no longer rely on beer to get me through, I simply avoid going out and meeting people full stop. This is ... far from ideal.

The lure of drink and drugs to help smooth over the social jagged edges that so many autistic people endure is strong, and it's something that's rarely discussed, even within the autistic community. Expecting autistic people to not rely on these two things to help us cope with the impossible expectations of 'going out' seems to me to be looking at the problem the wrong way around. Once again, the onus is completely on the autistic person to do what they can to fit in with a hostile system – who can blame us for finding solace in the bottom of a bottle? Much better would be a world where my recommendations in Chapter 2 were followed, where the 'going out' itself was modified or managed differently to permit autistic people to actually enjoy it too.

Away from the social travails of university, much of academia is fairly ideal for some aspects of the autistic experience. The fact that further study into more and more specific fields is part and parcel of university work makes it highly suitable for autistic people who maintain close focus on very precise special interests. It seems to me that managing to secure a degree in a course that's a genuine special interest is something of a victory, as it means that the hours of time poured into it will result in a tangible reward – a degree certificate and the promise of perhaps even deeper dives into the subject at post-graduate level.

I was a huge fan of the idea of staying at university indefinitely, insulating myself from the terrifying world off campus – as Dr Venkman (Bill Murray) states so baldly in the film *Ghostbusters*, 'You've never worked in the private sector: they expect results.' Staying at university would protect me from this. Although my diagnosis was still over ten years away, I already knew that I'd struggle in a work environment from my brief and awful forays into working at supermarkets and fast-food places as a student. As a result, I took a master's degree in English Literature, and attempted to secure funding for a PhD (something about psychogeography in the work of George Gissing, if I remember correctly). Perhaps wisely, the Arts Council decided that this was the last thing the world needed, and I was out of university, thrust into the world of work, knowing full well it was going to end very badly, as it proved to.

The interplay between education and autism is a fascinating one. In so many ways they go hand in hand: after all, autistic people are often very keen learners (especially when the topic is right) and almost every single autistic person I've met values knowledge and understanding very highly. We often have the tools needed to become exceptional learners (and teachers, much of the time) – a monotropic focus on details, a love of thoroughness, hyperlexia – and yet school and university are so frequently the worst time of our lives. Something is going horribly wrong here, and I believe that it's little more than a stubborn refusal on the part of our education systems to be flexible and compassionate. Our rigid services, so wedded to tradition and old-fashioned ideals, are failing autistic students time and time again. Despite small gains seen here and there, it feels that there's still a very long way to go before the whole education system in the UK could be classed as 'autism-friendly'.

6

EMPLOYMENT AND OTHER HAZARDS

DOES AUTISM WORK?

Until recently I've pretty much always worked in an actual workplace. Apart from for a very brief period in 2005 after finishing my expensive and possibly pointless master's degree, I've always held down a job and dutifully gone into work every morning or evening, trying to earn enough to survive in the world. But now, five years after my autism diagnosis, I'm self-employed and stay at home every day.

The two things are connected.

I first realised that the world of work might not be well aligned with my personality when I was fourteen and starting my first job. It was as ridiculously twee and cute as any first job has the right to be – working in a little pet shop called Paddy's Pets (I never found out where the 'Paddy's' bit came from; the owner was called Roger). It was a small, independent enterprise, filled with nooks, crannies and strange smells; my job, for eight hours every Saturday, was to stock shelves, sweep the floors and clean out the hamsters. Occasionally I'd have to work the till and actually communicate with customers. And I hated it.

There was, I realise now, nothing at all wrong with the job. The owner was kind and the other employees were pleasant. The tasks were easy enough, and I got to play with cute little rodents and small birds. I even got paid. Despite all of this I was miserable. At the time (and for about twenty years afterwards) I assumed the reason was that I must be terminally lazy and work-shy, and I tried hard to push through this apparently toxic aspect of my personality. I felt ashamed for struggling with such a simple, low-stakes job, especially as I watched my friends at school throw themselves into their part-time jobs, saving up for cars for when they passed their test. For me, the concept of working enough to be able to buy an actual vehicle was laughable. I could barely handle one shift.

The problem was that I was just so anxious all the time. I was petrified of interacting with customers and constantly bewildered by the various little jobs I had to complete. I was getting A and B grades at school but couldn't for the life of me remember how the till worked, which filled me with embarrassment. When I could remember the jobs I had to complete, I'd be scared of doing them wrong – not because of paranoia, but because I often *did* get them wrong, even when they were really straightforward. For the life of me I just couldn't understand why I found this all so difficult when I was finding English essays, French exercises and geography tests so easy. My ability to plan out my working day was non-existent, and by about 2 p.m. in the afternoon I'd be so ridiculously tired that I'd feel I was drifting off to sleep on my feet. But I had no frame of reference. My only recourse was to assume that either everyone felt this way or (and this was more likely) I was a lazy bum who deserved everything he got.

The result of this, and I'm sure it's widely applicable to a great many autistic and other neurodivergent people, is that the world of work provokes a general sense of uselessness and a severe lack of self-esteem. It feels much more hostile than it otherwise should, as so much is simply insurmountable. Constantly feeling overwhelmed and unable to cope with the working day is corrosive. It is amazing that I managed to sustain this until the age of thirty-eight – after all, that's nearly a quarter of a century of feeling inadequate, swamped by and afraid of my day-to-day routine.

Data shows that only around 22 per cent of autistic adults are in any kind of work, including part-time or casual. This data is probably pretty flawed, in that there are almost certainly thousands of undiagnosed autistic people who, for the same reason that they're undiagnosed, are able to manage (at least for now) the world of employment. But even taking these individuals into account, it's clear that too many autistic people find working an impossibility. Without work it's very difficult to maintain independence or a decent quality of life. As such, huge numbers of autistic adults have to either rely on their parents or the whims of whatever government they live under. This is not a good situation.

There are a multitude of factors that contribute to these terrible statistics; some would be surprisingly easy to counter, if only there were a concerted effort and will to make employment more accessible for the neurodivergent community. Sadly, to date, any attempts to make workplaces 'autism-friendly' have been extremely patchy and variable in quality. Things do seem to be improving, but progress currently makes glaciers look hasty and reckless. So, for anyone reading this who happens to be in a position of power, able to affect change on a large scale, let's begin by considering the workplace itself.

THE HORRORS OF THE WORKPLACE

As I've mentioned several times already I'm 6 foot 7, and as such I'm a spot too tall to fit properly into the world. I can't sit comfortably on trains or aeroplanes, I can't wash up or iron a shirt without hurting my back bending over, and my head is a mass of scar tissue from repeatedly bumping it on door frames, light fittings and those dangling signs advertising 50 per cent off in supermarkets. I therefore feel like a peculiarity, an outsider, compared with everyone else who happily exists in a world that fits. Being neurodivergent is a similar type of 'othering'. In the same way as my house was clearly designed for people of average height, the world's infrastructure and society as a whole are designed for neurotypicals. The places we work are no exception.

The work environment, just like the schools discussed in the previous chapter, is naturally hostile to autistic people. This is not on purpose (or at least I hope it's not!); it's simply a by-product of autistic people being so indistinct and ill-defined on everyone's radar as to be essentially invisible. Autistic people have very specific needs that, if met, would make environments more manageable. The trouble is that these needs are barely even known about, let alone acknowledged.

Non-autistic people have demands within their work environment. Of course they do – after all, they're human and have preferences regarding light quality, temperature, comfort and so on. Thanks to this, a large number of workplaces in the UK, and many more in countries inclined to be warmer, such as parts of the USA, will have air conditioning as standard. These thrumming machines appear in office buildings all over, with the purpose of cooling the work environment down to a 'suitable' range that best suits the majority of the folks who work there. No one questions this, and it's usually seen as a very good thing.

As I said, no one *ever* questions this.

Then an autistic person asks for an environmental adaption to suit *their* needs, and they're met with blank faces, confusion and – in particularly uncharitable moments – accusations of being 'needy' and 'awkward'. But where's the difference? Neurotypicals exist in a world that's carefully designed to meet their needs – why shouldn't autistic people have adjustments to meet theirs?

Temperature is one of these variables. It's due to the sensory sensitivity that's a defining feature of autism –

you may have noticed that it keeps coming up; in fact, most of the examples I'm about to give are fundamentally based on this sensitivity as it forms, after all, a very large part of our experience. Huge numbers of autistic people have smaller temperature ranges that they're comfortable in, in comparison to the ranges deemed acceptable by neurotypicals. On top of this, the ranges may be at the cooler end of the scale for some, or at the warmer end for others. Thanks to this, a lot of autistic people will find the temperature at their workplace – carefully regulated by the neurotypical majority – to be uncomfortable.

I can't stress this enough. I'm one of those who prefer a cooler atmosphere: around 18 to 19°C is ideal for me. The thing is, if the thermometer starts nudging towards 20°C or – God forbid – 21°C, I'll feel so desperately uncomfortable that my symptoms could be mistaken for serious illness. My energy leaks away, drained by the heat, my head gets stuffy and slow, and my skin feels stifled and smothered. It's an unpleasant feeling, and if I'm forced to stay in such an environment (I remember this happening a lot when I worked in fast food) it's guaranteed I'll get a bad headache and nausea. Naturally, my productivity suffers as a result.

This is why I always have a window open. It doesn't matter if it's snowing. Unless the temperature is in deep minus figures, which are exceedingly unusual in the British climate, that window is thrown open and the life-giving fresh air is encouraged to flow around the room, boosting my mood and preventing me spiralling into terrible discomfort. It's also why I've a desk fan trained upon me, even in February. It's as if I'm a very overworked computer processor and graphics card; I need constant cooling otherwise I start to break down. And this counts for the outside world, too. I've had several holidays in hot parts of the world, such as Turkey and Tunisia, and though I enjoy the feeling of warm sun on my skin, I'm pretty much perpetually miserable (or at least very stressed) by the ambient heat, especially if it's similarly humid. When the UK experiences its heatwaves, I essentially hibernate with a big fan and bowls of ice from the freezer until the temperature starts to drop again.

If you're an employer you need to be aware of the potential impact of temperature on your autistic staff. Offer to instal a fan on their desk, or ask if they'd like to be closer to the air conditioning. Alternatively, if their sensitivity works the other way around, is it possible to fix a small heater in their workspace to take the edge off that nasty cold breeze? These are easy fixes, and relatively cheap to boot. They should offer an immediate improvement.

And then there's light. This is frequently created by long, buzzing strip lights. These are fine for plenty of people, who don't notice the sound they make, but for autistic people they're evil. The buzzing is so insistent and relentless that after about twenty minutes in their company, I'm ready to rip the things off the ceiling and jump on them like an angry cartoon character. It's a common source of community with us autistics that we're able to 'hear' electricity. I knew from a very early age whether the television in the lounge was on standby, even from a distance. Many autistic people report being able to hear their phone charging, a kind of low hum that sneaks into our heads no matter what we do.

Then there's the light these things give off: somehow it's totally incompatible with neurodivergent brains. There's a kind of flicker – a lack of consistency – that has none of the charm of a sputtering candle and all of the misery of a torch repeatedly flashed directly into the retinas. At best this type of illumination is distracting; at worst it's actively harmful, causing headaches, eye strain and mood changes, and sometimes even leading to meltdowns.

If your workplace has strip lights I can pretty much guarantee that any autistic staff will absolutely hate them. I found my hatred was, for many years, entirely subconscious. It took real effort on my part to correlate my bad moods and even worse headaches with being in rooms that had these lights. One of the reasonable adjustments I got at work, when I was still a teacher, was an upgrade to the lights in my classroom, and the difference was amazing. The new lights were designed to emulate daylight and were completely silent, and the frequency of my head pain reduced significantly.

Interestingly, both of these issues – heat flexibility and lighting – might help non-autistic people too. Plenty of these people struggle with migraines brought on by poor-quality lighting, and I can't pretend that neurotypicals are such a monolith that they all enjoy the same ambient temperature. Employers adapting their workspaces to provide flexibility to temperature and healthier lighting would undoubtedly improve the lives of all of their employees, not just the neurodivergent ones.

Away from sensory issues, there's the nightmare of hot-desking. Thankfully, this is a practice that I've never had to endure, but it's apparently increasingly popular. If you haven't experienced it, it involves employees in office-based employment not having a set desk or space that's 'theirs'. Whereas traditionally an office worker would have their work space set up with their computer, a picture of their family, a few necessary stress toys and a pile of dirty coffee mugs, now it's increasingly common for an employee to rock up to work with their laptop to find that their favourite spot – maybe the one with the nice draught or near the radiator – is taken up by Kevin from accounting. This is bad enough for people generally, but for autistic employees it's nothing short of disastrous.

Work is stressful. On top of all the sensory aspects I've so far outlined in this chapter, there are the social issues and problems with hierarchies, instructions and more. As establishing a nice, rigid routine is so often an autistic person's response to extreme stress, stripping them of that is enormously damaging: how can anyone establish a decent set routine if they're going to be sitting in a different part of the office every day?

In my working life I've had to deal with a very similar issue, which any teachers who are reading this will recognise – suddenly being forced to teach in a different classroom. My classroom at my last job as a teacher was my haven, a sanctuary that, despite being filled all too often with a bunch of noisy kids demanding to be taught stuff, was still 'home'. My computer was set up precisely how I liked it – good, sharp resolution on the monitor (I can't abide fuzzy graphics), desktop folders where I wanted them, mouse sensitivity just right. My desk was a wonderland of precisely controlled chaos, with piles of paperwork representing the geological strata of my career, with the papers at the bottom of the piles often four or five years old and essentially forgotten, fossilised memos from an earlier era. My shelves were full of my own books and a variety of LEGO sets, most of which I'd built at my desk during lunch hours. It was as happy a space could be at work, and when a lesson was over and a free period began, I'd visibly sink with relaxation into my spinny chair, fan blowing into my face, hair stirred by it like in a shampoo commercial.

And then, out of the blue, I'd be dragged from this room and forced to teach in a room I'd never been in before. Sometimes this would be to cover a teacher who was off sick. Other times it would be because the timetable was so byzantine and unfathomable that my own room would be taken for a textiles class or something similarly illogical and impractical, forcing me to teach my class in an art or music room. Whatever the reason, it always edged my personal meltdown-o-meter deeper into the red. I would boot up the computer to be greeted by a monitor resolution of 800x600, as if the usual teacher enjoyed using it to play video games from the mid-1990s. My eyes screaming in horror, I'd discover the mouse tracked on screen at roughly the pace that continents move. The class would arrive, a shrill roar of potential energy, and I'd feel the panic beginning to mount in the front of my brain. The unfamiliar walls and disturbing lack of colourful, comforting LEGO houses and vehicles would begin closing in on me, and the heat and strange humidity of the room, and terrifying lack of a fan, would see me starting to sweat with more than just fear.

It may sound hyperbolic but my reaction to being shunted out of my room was always extremely negative and, unfortunately, uncontrollable. I couldn't resist this panic any more than I could resist feeling anxious before an important exam. Obviously, I'd always get through it – luckily I never succumbed to a full meltdown (though it was often a very close call) but I'd feel the after-effects linger in my system for hours, often even reaching into the next day. It will come as no surprise that the moment I was offered reasonable adjustments at work as a result of being diagnosed (nine years into my career), I begged for them to never make me leave my room again. They agreed, and for a pleasant year or so I was only ever in my room, my haven, my safe space. In 2020 this changed, as the pandemic hit and all existing rules and practices were thrown out. I lasted only a few days before I had to quit. My autistic self couldn't handle the new reality.

So, I've some understanding of the problem of hot-desking.

Of course, there's one answer to these issues, and it's a solution that's been brilliantly stress-tested over the last few years thanks to Covid: working from home. I cannot speak for all autistic people, but I think working from home is a pretty huge positive for us. What could be a more controlled, safe space than a person's own home? How better to handle the strains of commuting than not having to commute in the first place? What's more effective at removing the need for pointless, deeply stressful small talk in the corridors by the photocopier than not having colleagues anywhere but on a computer screen?

Although many decry the damage home-working has done to the social biosphere of the workplace, as an autistic person I can happily decry the social biosphere itself and welcome the opportunity to sit in my own living room to work, surrounded by as much LEGO and as many books as I could ever desire, with my own fan blowing directly into my face. The bad news is that the push to get people back into offices will most likely destroy many happy autistic employees' routines and attachments to workspaces that are finally suitable for them. If society is going to do the right thing, and make employment accessible for neurodivergent people, then home-working needs to remain on the table.

DOING A GOOD JOB

I've always been terrified of being criticised. It's unclear where this began, or why I've such a strong emotional reaction whenever anyone even implies the tiniest criticism. When the reviews for this book start coming in, you'll find me hiding under a duvet somewhere refusing to read them.

It's always been this way, for as long as I can remember, and my reaction to any form of negative attention is likely to be extreme. Some of my most vivid memories of childhood revolve around this. I remember standing in the queue for lunch at primary school when I was probably about eight years old. My memory insists that the headteacher of the school appeared by me in the queue – as a teacher I now realise she was invoking the ancient right of 'pushing in' the queue thanks to her status as an educator – and said to me, apropos nothing at all, 'You've been nothing but trouble since you started here.'

Now, we must all bear in mind that I was perhaps the most inoffensive student you can imagine. My response to the stresses and strains of school was to blend in to the background so far that I was invisible against the paint on the walls. The idea that any teacher could accuse me of being 'nothing but trouble' was absolutely ridiculous. But my eight-year-old brain did not consider this and it hurt so badly, and I took it so deeply to heart, that here I am, thirty years later, reporting the incident to you. Reality and common sense would suggest that the headteacher had either mistaken me for someone else (though it does make you wonder who the poor kid was that she'd mistaken me for), or that she'd actually said something different – perhaps ambiguous – that my brain skewed into something extremely negative.

It's possible that a reasonably common neurodivergent trait is at work here, one that some autistic people, and others with ADHD, report as being a particular burden on their lives. It's called Rejection Sensitivity Dysphoria (RSD), and I use the word 'burden' very purposefully. Usually, I endeavour to be as positive about neurodivergency as possible, and I genuinely see an awful lot to be optimistic about. However, when it comes to RSD I find it very difficult to see the good side. It's a truly damaging trait that has brought me nothing but misery all my life and, along with executive dysfunction, is by far the 'feature' of being neurodivergent that disables me the most. Before I explain how it works, can I just point out that word 'sensitivity'. Once again, we see a trait of autism built around an oversensitivity to a stimulus – in this case rejection or criticism. If autism has a 'grand unifying theory', as some suggest (with monotropism being a popular contender), then perhaps it's this intense sensitivity to *all* input that lies at its heart.

Rejection Sensitivity Dysphoria is the collective term for a set of reactions to any kind of negative attention, seemingly no matter how minor or inconsequential. The reactions can be pretty extreme, which is especially noticeable when the criticism or rejection that spawned them is very tiny, and it can be a major contributor to autistic meltdown. It's not limited to a person just being rejected, although that's a large part of it. Any kind of negative interaction can cause a disproportionate response, from being criticised for something, to being ignored or simply overlooked in some way. I find that probably 80 per cent of my negative feelings stem from this in some way, which raises the weird possibility of how happy-go-lucky I might be if it weren't for RSD. And I've no means of controlling it – or at least no way that I've yet discovered. It simply *is*, and it squats in my mind like a malevolent goblin, constantly needling me with reminders of how many ways people can hate me.

The thought process is hard to decipher as it all happens so quickly, but I'll approximate it as being something like this:

1. A stimulus occurs – maybe a person in earshot says something ambiguous like, 'Yeah, I'm not a fan either.'
2. My brain interprets this *immediately* as a judgement on me, my character and my physical appearance.
3. It becomes clear that they were, in fact, referring to some other issue … maybe a brand of coffee or a flavour of doughnut or something.
4. My brain refuses to return to its prior state of calm, despite assurances that I've not been horribly critiqued. It continues to fret about the whole situation for hours, seemingly still convinced it was all directed at me.

It has always seemed to me that there's an unholy alliance of two or maybe three autistic traits colliding in interestingly unreasonable ways here: the jumping-to-conclusions nature of an autistic brain that has been forced to read implication into everything they hear (thanks to the neurotypical addiction to never saying anything plainly), combined in a grim cocktail with the kind of autistic inertia that makes us so slow to move on or change path.

The result of all of this has many faces. First of all it's simply tiring. Imagine dealing with this all the time.

Imagine that one time where you actually *had* done something wrong at work and were worried about it, and you saw your boss talking to *their* boss, occasionally glancing across at you, maybe pointing at you, possibly occasionally snarling in your direction. You'd feel very nervous, very worried, and for pretty good reason – after all, all of the signs are there that you're about to be in trouble for whatever it was that you did. Now imagine that your brain had the ability, as well as boundless enthusiasm, to fabricate most of this evidence (the pointing, the glancing, the snarling), and then apply it to nearly every single interaction you've ever witnessed between any co-workers or colleagues, *even when you'd done nothing wrong*. That's RSD, and it's exhausting just to think about it.

Second, it makes you very insecure and drains your confidence. This is no good in the workplace, especially when you're neurodivergent. If you're autistic, chances are that there are many things competing to make you feel inadequate and poorly suited for your job. It's likely you'll feel socially excluded, for example; as we'll see shortly, there will also be a constant terror that you've misunderstood instructions or orders. Adding RSD into this already volatile mixture is going to make a person even less likely to excel in their work, and has the added effect of making some kind of mental illness almost inevitable, be it severe anxiety or full-blown depression.

Third, and most insidiously, there are those times where your paranoia proves itself to be well grounded, when your fears are realised and you get a boatload of criticism descend into your head from the heights of senior leadership. This has happened to me perhaps three times in my life (though I expected it probably a thousand times), and each time it fed my RSD, giving it more authority, and making me less and less able to rationalise myself out of it – after all, it was right that one time! I was once absolutely destroyed by a head-teacher, in my third year of teaching, because my work had suffered as a result of declining mental health. She verbally attacked me for a solid five minutes, in front of staff and parents at a sports day, confirming all of my RSD fears that I had experienced all year.

I left the school at the end of that term, still in shock. I now know that the head was receiving reports of my struggling to manage my job for a period of time but, rather than approaching me and checking I was OK, had let it bottle up and eventually explode in my face. This, if I may be so bold, is not the best way to look after your staff and serves as a reasonable example of how a hidden disability can lead to truly awful outcomes in the work-place. It has given me a deep mistrust of authority, and it proved to the RSD always lurking in my mind that yes – they probably do think you're doing a terrible job.

The lesson to be learned here – and I truly believe you'd be doing humanity a favour in general, not just neurodivergent people – is that if you have concerns about a colleague or feel that an employee isn't doing their usual standard of work, then you tell them. With a focus on positives and a 'How can I help?' attitude, it's possible that the potential RSD that any of your neuro-divergent staff may have to handle can be mitigated, if not entirely eliminated. If my headteacher, or line manager, had spoken to me earlier about my performance dropping (or if six-monthly rather than annual performance reviews were the norm), I'd have been in a position to open up about my difficulties. Admittedly, I didn't know at that time that I was neurodivergent, but it's possible the discussion could have opened up that possibility. At the very least it would have prevented the growing pressure of discontentment that my employer had for me, and stopped it from exploding in front of parents on what should have been a happy day. Rejection Sensitivity Dysphoria is a difficult thing to manage, and I wouldn't suggest that these measures would have 'cured' me in any way, simply that they would have stripped my RSD of its greatest weapon: the sneering voice whispering, '*I told you so …*'.

INSTRUCTIONS, ORDERS AND OTHER AMBIGUITIES

With social interactions, we do most of our learning (usually the hard way, involving bullying, fights, being ostracised from all other human beings … that kind of thing) early on, throughout our school days. Social stakes are high but – luckily – we're not dependent on our success to pay the rent or buy food. We have the space to make mistakes and, although the impact can be enormous at the time, we can often bounce back from negative school experiences reasonably well. Things change, however, when we reach our mid-twenties. The unwritten rules in a place of work can be just as arcane, illogical and downright unreasonable as those in the school playground. The problem is, if you get these wrong – even once – you can find yourself turfed out of the job and in dire financial trouble.

Let's talk about the one that always tripped me up: taking time off sick. In the UK we're allowed to get ill. I understand that over the Atlantic in the USA, being ill at work is seen as some kind of crime and the likelihood of getting sick pay is very low, but here in northern Europe it's understood that sometimes fate will wreck your day and make you come down with something nasty, and that you don't deserve to go hungry or lose your job as a result.

Or so they say.

You see, that may be what the rules state; it may well be written in the law; but how it actually transpires in the real world is a very different thing indeed. Sure, you'll get your sick pay, and when you return from a nasty bout of flu your desk will still be there (unless they're hot-desking, in which case you may as well take another week off), but is it really OK to get sick? The absence policy may state that you can take off *x* number of days a year, but depending on your workplace, your employers' attitude towards you if you go ahead and max out your allowance may get very frosty indeed. This is the kind of thing that autistic people can really struggle with. One autistic individual I spoke to told of an awful situation whereby they were berated at their desk, in front of colleagues, for taking off some days for migraines. They were told that the problem was that they were separate days, rather than a chunk of days together. As 'unwritten rules' go, that's a real kick in the teeth.

Because of the nature of autism and masking, as well as the prevalence of comorbidities like epilepsy, Ehlers–Danlos syndrome and migraines, having to take some days off every year is almost inevitable. I too suffer terrible migraines, which I chalk up mostly to my constant anxiety and sensory sensitivity – both of which are intrinsically linked to being autistic – and when I was working for an employer, rather than being self-employed as I am now, I usually ended up using my full allowance of sick days every single year. As the rules state that we're allowed a certain number of days, generally speaking the autistic response is that that many days off must be, by default, absolutely fine. Perhaps it's a bonus if an employee *doesn't* take off all those days, but if they do – well, it's allowed and therefore everything is fine. This is the logical take. It makes sense. But it's not the reality.

The reality is that there are rules that are not codified into law, that differ between different organisations and even individuals, and that you're *not allowed to ask about beforehand*. Instead, a strange game of chance is played, where every illness and required time off work involves risk, like deciding to hit rather than stick on a really high-stakes game of blackjack, as you may find yourself angering your employer for being off sick too much. This won't be connected to the number of days to which you're legally entitled – instead it will be based on your employers' general attitude to sickness, and their overall compassion. It's not something that sits well with many autistic minds, as it simply doesn't make any sense. What's the point in having rules and quotas and established limitations if they're meaningless and overridden by nebulous arbitrary lines? But this is the way things are done, and autistic people are already struggling too much to be able to start challenging such a hopeless status quo.

There's ample ambiguity in the day-to-day running of a workplace too. Everything from breaktimes to deadlines comes with an extra layer of mythology that can only be learned by chatting to our more-established colleagues, if at all. Breaktimes are thirty minutes? Sure, but it's best to be back at your desk in twenty otherwise Dirk in management will think you're lazy. No requirement to bring in birthday cake for everyone on your birthday? Great, except if you don't you'll be viewed as a social pariah for the rest of your time here. Dirk tells you to get a job done by the end of the day on Friday? Oh, he actually means 10 a.m. on Thursday for reasons that literally no human being could ever determine. When I was teaching, the school day ended at 3 p.m. and we were expected to be in school until 4 p.m. That's fine, except if you left at 4 p.m. on the dot, then you were openly viewed with disdain and seen as being somehow lesser than those teachers who kept the candle burning at both ends, working until 6 p.m. and beyond. This never seemed fair to me.

Schedules and deadlines are pretty good, really. I struggle to meet them sometimes (executive dysfunction once again rears its head), but I appreciate the idea and they genuinely do help me cope with the world. But my God, if you want an autistic person to abide by a deadline, tell us the truth! Tell us exactly when the very latest time would be that will avoid us being viewed as lazy bums. Don't imply it. Don't tell us a time that will actually anger you, should we abide by it. Just be honest and say you expect the job to be done by the time you actually expect it to be done.

Once again, in actually setting all of this down on paper, I find myself shaking my head at the bizarre ways that neurotypical people dance the dance of communication. So many things are implicit, hidden and vague it's a wonder that anything actually gets done. This type of approach most certainly doesn't work for the vast majority of autistic people and so we find ourselves looking at another opportunity to create a more equitable workspace, where small (and usually free) changes can improve the lives of autistic employees by a huge margin:

- Make sure you're totally transparent about your requirements, including deadlines, as set out above. But also ensure that your instructions and demands leave nothing to be inferred. If you want the work to be presented in a certain way, then say so. If you need more than one copy, explain that. If the equipment needs putting in a specific location, tell us. If the coding has to be completed before anything else, then make that priority clear. It's not insulting to be totally clear to autistic people; it will almost always be appreciated, so long as it isn't accompanied by, say, a patronising tone of voice.

- Make sure that all instructions for any kind of task (as far as possible) are provided in writing as well as verbally. Many autistic people can struggle to retain verbal information – after all, we can be so busy trying to maintain our mask and look you in the eye that you might as well be mowp-mowping like the teacher from *Charlie Brown* as far as we're taking anything in. Put it in an email so that we can scour it for all required information at our leisure. This has the bonus effect of helping us get organised, as we can arrange our emails into folders, use the fancy little multicoloured flags to help prioritise and so on. Honestly, email may well be the Devil in many ways, but its ability to keep me organised is second to none.

- Reminders can go a long way for neurodivergent staff. In my last job, one of my 'reasonable adjustments' was to request 'judgement-free' reminders on key tasks. It's another way to tackle executive dysfunction, though the 'judgement-free' bit is really important – don't begrudge reminding us, or make it sound like the need for a reminder is a sign of failure.

- Make sure almost nothing comes as a surprise. Some people may thrive on the thrill of sudden demands on a Monday morning, but the vast majority of autistic people do not. If you want something doing, make sure we're given plenty of notice. This is to help avoid the problem of

inertia and slow attention swapping, but also
neatly sidesteps the possibility of a PDA
response, which is pretty handy.

I hope it's clear by now that most of the adjustments that can be made in the workplace are easy to implement, either very cheaply or totally free, and mostly revolve around the idea of basic compassion. Nothing that I've mentioned in this chapter is out of the reach of the vast majority of employers, and just imagine how much easier things would be for the neurodivergent minority if such advice were taken and applied consistently. Perhaps we would see a gradual increase in the proportion of autistic people able to access work and maintain financial independence – what an excellent outcome that would be. But the power lies in the hands of the neurotypical. We autistics can shout about it until the proverbial cows come home, some of us can even write whole books about it, but nothing will change until the neurotypicals do.

OFFICE POLITICS AND HIERARCHY

Let me tell a little story about a job interview I once had. I'd been the head of the English department at my school for a few years, and had done pretty well. An opportunity came up to be seconded to the senior leadership team for a term or so, and I applied. In the interview I was asked why I wanted the job. Now, you must understand that at this point I was friendly enough with my bosses that I'd habitually joke along with them, chat about nonsense; the kind of thing a person does when they know someone pretty well and you get on well. In the interview, I therefore felt like I was in a safe position to be myself: after all, they'd known me for years and we'd been to the pub together at least once. I'd even made them laugh before.

I leaned back a little in my chair and explained that, following my diagnosis of autism, I wanted to stretch myself to prove to myself I could still do leadership roles. I told them I was too prone to hiding away in my classroom, and that I wanted to push myself to get out there more and get involved in the school. I was typically self-deprecating when I said, 'I don't want to end up a weird little hermit hiding in my cupboard when people knock on the door'. It was a joke, but one that was firmly built on what I thought was common knowledge about my personality. I knew I was seen as a bit of a parochial figure – a bit distant, perhaps – and I knew that any employer would probably want their middle managers to be a little more visible.

Boy, had I misjudged the situation.

Later that day the deputy head came in and apologetically informed me that I hadn't got the position, with the reason partly being that I'd come across as too negative about my own capabilities, too self-deprecating. I had, in short, horribly misunderstood the rules of engagement. In being open, honest and blunt about my own failings, I'd alienated the interviewers; after all, the rules of job interviews are that you make yourself sound as good as you possibly can, almost to a level that's absurd. I suppose the old joke of replying to the question 'What is your biggest weakness?' with yet more positives should have warned me about this phenomenon, but I'd been lulled into a false sense of security by my relationship with those sitting opposite me. I see now that I should have acted rather like I'd never met them, been standoffish and aloof, and answered with sincere exaggeration – but it's all too late.

The fact is I blew it, and looking back with what I now understand about autism, I can begin to see exactly why it is that it happened. You see, autistic people (generally speaking, as always) often seem to have something of a blind spot when it comes to authority figures: bosses, the police, the government, teachers. Why this is seems open to debate, but I have my theories.

I've always said that if I were ever to meet someone truly important – the King, say, or a president of some kind – then the likelihood of me saying or doing something inappropriate is set at around 100 per cent. I don't know why, but to me anyone in a position of real authority is still, first and foremost, a person. Thus, I think if I met the King my brain would default to: 'Here's a friendly seeming older gentleman – feel free to make jokes about the weather and ask how he's getting on since the death of his mother.' I wouldn't be doing this to appear 'cool' or rebellious in some way; more that the concept that it's somehow wrong to treat such a person as entirely normal wouldn't occur to me at all. I would have to be reminded, and even then I'd struggle. To put it bluntly, the chances of me accidentally farting in front of the King and then joking about it are limited only by the chances of me ever actually meeting the King.

Authority and hierarchy are social constructs and, as I've been at pains to point out, autistic people have our own, different, culture that doesn't seem to include it. I'm not saying that autistic people are true egalitarians (well, I almost am – it's just there's not enough evidence for this yet) but that we certainly don't seem to care very much for such arbitrary ideas. I think it is fair to say that many autistic people see authority as something that has truly got to be earned, that it's not enough to simply 'be' in charge – you must have demonstrated good reasons why this is the case. And even then, being in charge doesn't make you any different from a normal human being.

In practice this leads to lots of tricky situations that vary in terms of their severity. At one end it can lead to a lack of fear that may prove to be valuable and appreciated by the powerful figure; an employee, say, who 'says it like it is' and ends up building a positive relationship with the boss built on a lack of obsequious kowtowing. At the other end, however, it can lead to displays that might be viewed as 'lacking respect', which are likely to have the opposite effect. Worse, in situations where the person in authority has no knowledge of the autistic person, we might see situations spiral out of control very quickly – this is a real fear when the authority figure is a police officer. In these situations, an autistic person not displaying an appropriate level of fear and subservience could find themselves being challenged and ultimately arrested (or worse, in some parts of the world).

If you happen to be an employer, then it's good to be aware of this trait and adjust your expectations of how you might be treated by autistic employees accordingly. Too many autistic people get into too much trouble as a result of it, and I feel that it's well past time to ensure that autistic employees are understood, and that their general attitude to authority is no longer automatically assumed to be rudeness. There's a lot to be said for employers giving autistic people the benefit of the doubt, rather than viewing their behaviour through a neurotypical lens and misinterpreting what they see. Employers need to be more knowledgeable about how autism works, so that they're able to understand their neurodivergent employees and enable them to thrive.

After all, too many autistic people who want to work, and are physically able to do so, are out of work. This means we're much less able to support ourselves and live an independent life, and often all because our behaviour is just that tiny bit different from the established norm. Thousands if not millions of individuals are struggling to get by because too many employers lack any kind of understanding of what autism is. This is not a problem with the autistic community; it's a problem with the work community.

It rears its head dramatically in the strange theatre of job interviews, much like the one I outlined above. Neurotypical job interviews are a true obstacle course for autistic candidates, given how much stock is placed in soft social skills like eye contact, small talk, bravado/confidence and a good, appropriate sense of humour; it's almost as if job interviews are actively stacked against autistic people, when you look at them like that. Often it feels like you're being interviewed to see how much of a great buddy you'll be in the office, rather than for your skills and competence at the job, and this doesn't sit right with me, removing as it does such a vast swathe of neurodivergent candidates. There are simple accommodations that can be put into place:

- Allow interviewees to either see the location in advance, or allow them to be interviewed remotely so that the change of scenery and the stress of a new location don't throw them off.
- Allow them to see the questions in advance if they'd like to, and don't hold this against them. After all, many autistic people simply need a little more time to process questions and formulate answers.
- Don't make decisions based on a candidate's sociability, especially when that has nothing to do with the job description.
- Be honest in the advertisement: what level of experience is *really* required? Too often, employers will accept excellent candidates with little or no specific experience, despite the advert stating clearly that such experience is 'vital'. We autistics take language seriously, so we probably wouldn't even bother to apply if we didn't have the qualifications or experience demanded in the advert. This doesn't seem fair.

I spend a decent amount of time talking in workplaces about neurodiversity, explaining the workplace from an autistic perspective, to help companies and employers do better. I explain to them that they need to be clearer in their rules and expectations, that they need to make interviews more accommodating and that they should understand that autistic people are not magical data wizards. Every single time I find I have to start from scratch – from the absolute basics – because the knowledge simply isn't there. All too often I find employers and HR departments are still quoting *Rain Man*, and assuming that (a) they can't possibly employ autistic people and (b) they don't possibly have any autistic employees yet. Well, you can, and you almost certainly do.

When given appropriate support, autistic people are just as capable of earning a livelihood as anyone else, and when the vast majority of this support is as easy and cheap as 'slightly adjusted communication' or 'knowing how autism works', then is there really any excuse?

7

NOTHING SO STRESSFUL AS A REST

TRYING TO RELAX

In this chapter I'm likely to drift into discussing ADHD. The links between autism and ADHD are well known, in that they're often co-occurring and seem to complement each other in particular ways, but simultaneously absolutely bewildering as we still don't really know exactly how they're linked, or whether they may both be manifestations of some deeper singularity. The fact is, if a person is autistic, there's a fairly good chance they might be ADHD too (and if you're feeling expansive, feel free to throw dyslexia, dyscalcula and dyspraxia in there too). And so I make no apologies for the frequent crossovers in this chapter, which starts with a startling yet absolutely true fact.

I don't believe I've had a moment's true relaxation for at least ten years.

Autism is, for many, a whirlwind of anxiety. Everything I've already described to you adds to this maelstrom of nervousness – the constant sensory bombardment, the endless misinterpretation of others and their motives, the continuous issues with our executive function. Stress like this is not healthy, and it must contribute considerably to the sobering statistics around autistic people's shorter life expectancy. Being able to combat this stress and manage it successfully is therefore absolutely paramount. However, I simply cannot relax.

I know how to try to relax. I have, over the years, tried many different strategies to get my head to calm itself down and find a moment's peace. None of them have worked, or, if they did work for a time, they always stopped working – usually in the most inopportune ways.

I remember being in a state of constant high alert at school. I suppose this is why I found the breaks in routine for PE and science experiments so awful. Looking back, I feel that my whole body was tense much of the time – my muscles tight and unhappy, making the fluidity of movement necessary for sports impossible. It's interesting that one of the older traits of autism that doctors are still advised to look out for is stiff, almost robotic movement. I feel like this is often viewed as being a quirk of autism – a thing unto itself – rather than a symptom of stress. For me, as far as I display this trait at all, it's absolutely a result of stress-crushed muscles. However, I can't tell you what I'm worried about – not specifically, at least. My childhood was no picnic, but it wasn't as bad as it could have been. I have loving parents who did their best for me, and nothing terrible ever happened, so I'm unable to pin my endless tension on anything like that. The source of my stress was always, and remains, nebulous, unclear, abstract. I believe this is why it's so hard to combat.

Yet I've tried everything. As soon as I was allowed to I took the easy route of self-medicating with alcohol. Of course, in the short term this works brilliantly, and for a magical half-hour everything is more relaxed and serene. However, once this delightful but brief stage is over then everything becomes twice as bad and anxiety ratchets up even higher. No, booze is not the way to go, although it took me ten years to realise this. As an alternative, I poured a great deal of energy into meditation and mindfulness, acupuncture and even yoga. But none of these work, and I'll attempt to explain why.

I can achieve brief periods of mindfulness. However, managing this is like trying to hold back an avalanche with your arms – it's brave, but bloody pointless. Whenever I set out to 'do' a bit of mindfulness, I'll try to inhabit a quiet part of my brain and focus on the little things – I like looking at trees when I do this, for some reason, particularly their buds, twigs and leaves – while concentrating on my breathing. The problem is that my brain is like a busy apartment block where everyone is loud and noisy and horrible, and all of the walls are thin plaster. All of the little nooks and crannies of my mind are assaulted by an endless dirge of noise and activity from other parts of my brain, like trying to sleep while your neighbour – who really loves grime – is having the biggest party of their lives. For short bursts I can keep all of this noise back, bracing myself against it while I try to quietly consider the buds of the cherry tree, but it's useless, and before long the din and intensity of the rest of my brain bursts through the door with a four pack of beers, screaming.

My brain simply never shuts up. I've heard legends of people whose brains don't constantly talk to them, of people without an endless interior monologue, and I'm jealous. Rather than a serene blank of quiet, my brain is like a particularly disagreeable radio host, constantly filling the silence, terrified of 'dead air', forever barking into my consciousness with its pointless irrelevancies and observations – 'Oh look, there's a blue car. That car is quite different from that other blue car you just saw – you know, the one with the weird headlights – but it's also similar in a number of ways: first …'

I don't want to know any of this. I don't care about car colours, their number plates or the arrangement of house numbers on a street. I care little about the fact I've now passed five people in a row wearing a hat. I couldn't give one solitary shit about the way the tarmac on the pavement is patterned from years of being patched up. But try telling the DJ that. They don't want to hear it. As far as they're concerned, I need to know about all of this stuff, and the more I fight it, the more insistent they are.

I know that there are ADHD medications that will apparently assist me with this, but I'm currently two years into a waiting list for getting that diagnosis and I've got no hope of obtaining the medicine without it. So I'm left alone with my foolish, noisy head, doing my best to find ways to at least turn the volume down a notch or two. Much of it is ADHD talking – the relentless 'aware-ness' of everything that's happening, and the inability to disconnect from stimuli – but it's very interesting how autism interacts with this.

It lies in the nature of the things that I'm forced to notice – the car number plates and so on. This endless pattern-spotting is a key trait that many autistic people share. It's part of what makes some of us excellent at jobs involving data, numbers and programming, and my brain excels at it. The trouble is, rather like some neurological version of Gallup or YouGov, it's constantly collecting minute data on *everything* I pass, and if I'm honest I would really rather it didn't.

Pattern spotting *can* be very calming, in some situations. I remember having a method of soothing my anxious mind when I was a kid, sitting in the living room at home with my parents and sister. Like most families of the era (the mid-1990s), we had a VCR with an LCD display on it – you know the kind of thing, where time is represented by a collection of horizontal and vertical bars in the shape of an '8', with each bar lit to approximate the shape of numbers. Well, my brain devised a fun little distraction whereby I would see if the time displayed allowed me to count the vertical and horizontal bars alternatingly. So, the time 08:00 has sixteen verticals and only nine horizontals – this would be a failure – whereas the time 22:31 has eight verticals and nine horizontals – this would work. If it sounds ridiculous, that's because it is, but it was also extremely soothing. I could retreat into doing it if things got tense at home (as they did often, thanks to us not having much money) and, even better, the challenge updated every minute! Bargain.

Occasionally, like this, the intersection of autism and ADHD in terms of pattern spotting and the brain being constantly 'on' can work in our favour, especially in terms of our special interests. Once my noisy, chattering brain is aimed towards a key interest of mine, then the fact it never shuts up becomes a positive, and my internal monologue becomes the presenter of some tremendously fascinating documentary about the *Titanic* or the coalfields of north-west Leicestershire or whatever is the big thing of the moment. These are times that I can love my babbling little DJ, monologuing away.

But even this small comfort doesn't remove the fact that most of the time this endless internal voice is grating and exhausting. But the worst thing it can do – the absolute pits, as far as I'm concerned – is become self-absorbed. It's one thing when the narrative is constantly identifying the manufacturers of the cars around you, and another thing entirely when it's solemnly and brutally identifying all of your own internal fears, doubts and anxieties. I'm not saying that this is a uniquely neurodivergent thing, because it isn't. However, given that plenty of autistic people have this relentless pattern-spotting and these periods of hyperfixation, the experience is likely to be a lot more intense for us.

One example I can give is when I'm trying to relax, meditate or be mindful. If I do manage to find a moment of quiet in my brain, a corner of peace where the chaos and noise seem far away, it's only a matter of time before the rest of my brain finds me (I picture it almost scanning for signs of me, like a guard tower with a searchlight in a prison movie) and directs all of that hyperfocus, hyperfixation and chatter back onto me: 'Oh, there you are, trying to relax. Oh OK, well I can help keep an eye on your breathing – no that was too short, no, look, you're breathing weirdly now, stop thinking about breathing, OK, keep an eye on your breathing. Hey! What's going on with your heart there, was that a palpitation? Oh another, keep an eye on your heartbeat ...'

And so it goes.

It's interesting to me that a number of autistic people I know are what some might label 'hypochondriacs', based on the phenomenon I just described. I feel that the majority of people go through life without ever thinking too much about the way their body is operating – they're content to just run it into the ground at their own pace. However, I have this over-thinking and self-introspection happening all the time, the health equivalent of when you think too much about the way you're walking and end up moving in a weird, entirely alien manner as a result. As a consequence I spend too much time worried about the various sensations and throbs and beats and aches that my brain fixes its searchlight upon. It's not quite the same as interoception – the sense that informs us that we're hungry, or thirsty, or in pain, which is ironically often not entirely functional for some autistic people – as it's directed the other way; rather than listening to the signals my body sends, I'm fixated on all the sensations within my body, good, bad or indifferent. Interoception is useful and helps maintain human bodies. A hyperfixation on all of my internal systems is not so handy.

Every small ache becomes a potential problem. Every missed heartbeat is a potential heart attack. Every twinge in my stomach is potential food poisoning, and all because my internal monologue, already irritating when directed outwardly, is now focused internally and yet doesn't really know what to do with the glut of information it receives. As can readily be imagined, this doesn't help my endless anxiety.

It's interesting that this inward-pointing over-analysis can exist concurrently with what we call *alexithymia*, or a distinct difficulty in recognising our own moods and feelings. Many autistic people report struggling to identify what they're feeling or why they may be feeling it. Too many times to count I've found myself feeling generally uncomfortable in some hard-to-define way, but at a loss to hone it down with any precision. For example, it may be that something occurs that might cause some kind of envious feeling – someone I know gets some new LEGO or something – and I will, for a time afterwards, feel this vague disquiet. It's only after a little serious inner reflection and focus, often with the help of someone else, that I can realise that I'm actually feeling the emotion envy. So while I may be closely analysing the inner biology of my system, looking for flaws and potential issues in an overwrought, hyperfixated fashion, I may simultaneously be completely unable to identify that all of this is making me feel very worried, or nervous, or scared.

If you live or work with autistic people, and wonder why we can be so tightly wound and stressed, then it's worth considering whether this is a problem for them.

Being constantly anxious and 'switched on' in this way can be deadly, if unchecked, so do whatever you can to help us relax. One of the best things to do is remind us of things that have worked in the past. I can't speak for all autistic people, but I've found that when I'm really stressed, my mind blanks on those few things that can help me – a shower, listening to music – and having someone gently (don't forget the PDA!) prod me in that direction can be really useful.

If we're going to survive, it becomes vital to find some way of controlling this anxiety and stress when none of the standard methods work. Luckily, autistic people have a natural option to use for precisely such occasions – it's just a shame it's so socially unacceptable ...

STIMMING OURSELVES CALM

I've mentioned stimming a few times so far, but without truly explaining what it's all about. I'm not exaggerating when I say that understanding stimming is understanding a whole world of autistic experience, and where better to discuss it than in a chapter all about how we autistics manage our own moods and fears.

'Stimming' is an informal term that the autistic community seems to have agreed fits our need. The word has been around a while, seemingly coined in the 1970s as a shortening of 'stimulation' or 'stimulatory', and its use has exploded in the twenty-first century as it became commonly used to describe an integral part of the neurodivergent experience. It describes the physical and sometimes verbal actions that many, if not most, autistic people will utilise to help regulate our mood, rather like a safety valve that allows a release of pressure. These actions are usually repetitive in nature and very tactile, involving repetitive movements, sounds or the continued 'fiddling' with a small object – anything from a pen to a padlock. Sometimes there's an element of texture to it, so for example stroking a pleasantly soft toy or piece of clothing, but often it's more the movement itself that soothes. Autistic stimming is as varied as the autistic people who do it, but you may see anything from hand-flapping, rocking and foot-tapping to dancing, repeating words or clapping, or something else entirely.

A very interesting thing about stimming is its universal nature. Everybody stims, to some extent. You may well be sitting there – tapping your foot as you read, fiddling with the button on a ballpoint pen – scoffing at the idea that you'd ever do such a thing. I rest my case. It's a human response to stress or anxiety – a kind of burning off of that restless energy that our bodies seem to generate as a response to worrying about the gas bill. We stride backwards and forwards across the room as we engage in a difficult phone call, we rub our temples when concerned or play with our hair when worried. Because of this universality, each and every neurotypical should be able to empathise with the autistic community on this topic.

But generally speaking, they don't.

First, there's the very common issue of neurotypicals recognising an autistic trait as something they themselves do from time to time, and immediately assuming that this means the autistic person is 'making a mountain out of a molehill', as it were. Every autistic person who's openly autistic will recognise the phenomenon. We share, from a position of some vulnerability, one of the challenges we face, only to be met with a blithe statement along the lines of: 'Well, we all do that, don't we?' or 'I think that's something everybody does!'

It might be that the intent is to show solidarity, but the effect is always one of diminishing our difficulties, making us feel like we're moaning about something that other, stronger, better people just get on with. It's highly damaging to an autistic person's sense of self-worth, and it happens *all the time*. So the fact that stimming *is* recognisable to neurotypicals tends to weirdly warp into a source of embarrassment for them rather than a source of understanding. What neurotypical people need to hear and, more importantly, accept is that for autistic people, stimming is a much, much bigger deal.

I will have failed in my main objective if you've not, by now, come to understand the fact that autistic people exist at a far higher level of stress and anxiety on a daily basis compared with the neurotypical majority. Thanks to the constant over-stimulation from our sensory sensitivity and monotropic focus, and the social difficulties we wrestle with, we're always stressed out. We're always having that 'difficult phone call about the gas bill'. As such, we stim an awful lot more than you do.

I learned that stimming was 'bad' when I was a kid. I don't remember the specifics, but I can see the after-effects. All of my stims now are easy to hide, minor movements (unless I get really upset); I tend to wriggle my feet quite extravagantly when stressed, but thanks to my boat-like shoes, this movement is hard to notice if I'm at work or out and about. I also have a stim where I wriggle my hips; like a belly-dancer, I suppose, only much less graceful. Again, this is relatively easy to hide if I'm sitting behind a desk as I can keep my top half very still as I do it.

And so, like an archaeologist drawing conclusions about the past from the evidence of the present day, I can say with some certainty that I must have realised that I had to hide my stims at some point. Why else would they be so subtle, so 'inoffensive'? And it would make sense because so many autistic people have had their stims used against them. Stimming is among the most visible aspects of being autistic, so it stands to reason in this benighted world that it's one of the most frequent reasons why autistic people are bullied or otherwise badly treated.

Much autistic stimming *will* look different from the kinds of actions non-autistic people engage in. For this reason, seeing an autistic person stim, without knowing what's going on, is likely to cause confusion and consternation. I wish it didn't – I wish human beings were the kind of species who truly lived and let live, but we may as well be realistic. Autistic stimming is likely to trigger a reaction based on just how *different* it is from neuro-typical behaviour. We don't like difference, so autistic people learn very quickly (and often painfully) that their stims are not welcome here. Learning less obvious stims, or only stimming in private, becomes yet another aspect of autistic masking. And we all know how that eventually turns out.

It's therefore very important that autistic people have the freedom to stim however we need to, in order to help us regulate our stress levels, experience the world and even enjoy ourselves. After all, stimming is not all a doom-and-gloom response to terrible things; it can be a joyful, wonderful means of emoting and experiencing life. Many autistic advocates online, on Twitter and TikTok especially, have shared their stims with the world in an effort to raise awareness and understanding, so that autistic people can feel more and more confident in themselves. Often this includes stimming that's purely positive: the dancing and hand-flapping that accompanies exciting moments in life, the rhythmical movement of body parts to show appreciation or contentedness. Above all, when watching autistic people stim, I feel a sense of release and freedom that's hard to match, and so far removed from my restrained, buttoned-up stimming, born of years of conditioning.

Stimming is an integral part of autistic life, and one that's too often crushed and wrecked by neurotypical expectations. If you know an autistic person, in any capacity, then learn to allow us to express ourselves and stim.

If you see a stranger apparently stimming in the street, then give them the benefit of the doubt, remember that stimming exists and let them go about their day. Don't associate these movements and sounds with anything scary or strange; associate them with autistic people who have learned how to help themselves get through life, and with autistic people who have found a way to express their joy and sorrows. Associate them with the body language that's unique to autistic culture.

PLANNING IN ADVANCE

I became a teacher by accident. I'm deadly serious. For as long as I remember I've had absolutely no ability to plan long-term; the concept of setting a goal five years hence and steadily working towards it is as fanciful to me as the concept of setting off on a quest to drop a magic ring into a volcano. If I'm ever asked in interview, 'Where do you see yourself in five years' time?' my answer can only ever be, 'Hopefully, alive.'

I don't know exactly why this is. I've asked autistic people many times whether they feel the same way, and some do. But many don't. It seems that appreciable numbers of autistic people actually enjoy setting up long-term plans and carefully working towards them, which would actually fit with much of what we know about autism – this would be a clear result of, say, a long-term plan morphing into a special interest. Likewise, many ADHD people report having similar issues with long-term plans, which makes a lot of sense given the fact that ADHD is in part about focus drifting and being distracted by new stimuli. My gut feeling is that once again there's a little of both working here – in my case at least.

In either case, a discussion of planning certainly deserves a place in this book.

For me, looking into the future is distinctly myopic. I can reliably deal with looking ahead by perhaps a month, at most; a week feels nice and clear, and I'm able to predict and plan my comings and goings over that manageable timescale. Two or three weeks begins to feel murky, in a kind of fog. Anything over four weeks seems so impossible to predict with any level of accuracy that I seem to just give up, leaving it as a huge 'maybe' that I'm in no way able to consider in any detail. As an example, I'll use this book. Now, for those unfamiliar with the world of publishing (as I was until very recently), the process of taking a book from initial idea to being available in the shops often takes about two years or so, with the actual writing process itself being a relatively short period within that two years. This book had a six-month turnaround period in terms of getting it written to my own satisfaction (more time is given to external editors, of course). Six months is considerably longer than one month, as any mathematicians reading will know, and this presented a huge problem to me, as the eventual deadline for the book, for the majority of the time I was meant to be writing it, felt so far off in the gloomy fogs of time that I couldn't really comprehend it.

It was only as the deadline began to approach that it all started to make more sense, and accordingly my focus upon the task sharpened and my daily word count began to increase. The thing is, at no point was there a panic. I got the thing written with time to spare, after all, and without any real crisis. It's simply that my ability to visualise the endpoint of writing the book was non-existent for about 80 per cent of the time I was writing, and in that last 20 per cent I was so much more effective and focused. Much is made of how a lot of autistic and ADHD people end up doing the bulk of their work – whatever it may be – just before deadline hits, and I wonder if this is the reason. Often it's chalked up to procrastination and – well, the number of hours I played on *Minecraft* tells me that this is certainly a factor. But I think that my inability to clearly understand more distant targets and time scales is involved here too. The procrastination explanation would lead one to expect a period of mad panic and terror in those last weeks; instead, the opposite was true.

Once a book is written, it then enters a very prolonged period of tweaking and development. Edits have to be completed, of course, and the cover needs to be designed. People are approached to give glowing endorsements that will feature heavily on the front or back covers. Indexing has to be arranged if necessary and marketing organised. As I now enter that time period (as I write, publication is about eleven months away), the date of this book hitting the shelves is essentially mythical to me. I can no more envisage it happening than I can see myself strolling on the surface of Mars. The idea of holding this book in my hands in its finished, pristine form is so laughably remote and strange that in my everyday life, as I potter about doing my daily stuff, I cannot give it a moment's consideration. I can only treat it as a teenager might the idea of one day becoming a parent – as a vague and abstract possible future that I may one day experience.

No, as far as I'm concerned the future is a realm of mystery and wonder that I'll never actually reach.

There are interesting repercussions to having such a peculiar relationship with forward planning. It means that I find it hard to organise events or big moments. Unfortunately, being a parent contains an awful lot of these, from working out school placements and vaccine schedules, to planning birthday parties and nice Christmases. All I can say is that it's a *very* good job that in our case there are two parents to work out this stuff. Much is related to executive dysfunction. As you'll remember, executive dysfunction covers all of this administrative difficulty – not being able to prioritise effectively, struggling with decision making and so on – and also includes finding it hard to plan ahead. In everything I've read about the subject, this difficulty with planning has been seen as just another part of executive dysfunction. I'd say that in my case it's more compli-cated than that, and is closely entwined with my inability to envisage any future beyond a month hence. After all, how can you plan for a future that you literally cannot conceptualise? I wonder how many autistic or ADHD people would agree.

If you have a neurodivergent person in your life, I think it's really important to be aware of this particular set of difficulties. The problem is that the natural assumption made about those of us who have this 'future-blindness' is that we're generally ill-prepared and a bit useless at life. This fails to take into account the fact that (a) we cannot help it and (b) we may well be trying very hard to compensate for these 'shortcomings' but are still coming up lacking. As a result, the best thing that can be done is to show compassion and, as far as possible, help us out with the difficulties. I've found that my inability to imagine my book being out in the world has been helped by speaking with other writers, who can go over the practicalities of it all in more detail, helping me to envisage the experience. If you're able to assist practically, doing a bit of the person's planning for them, then all the better. As I say on a regular basis, autism is a disability; as a result of that we shouldn't feel bad for asking for help from those who *can* do these things.

So I find it hard to relax and I find it impossible to visualise the future in any meaningful way. As you may have already guessed, I'm therefore probably not the best person to set about trying to book a journey somewhere far off and exotic.

PLANES, TRAINS AND AUTOMOBILES

All modes of transport present a particular set of problems for autistic people. Each manages to set up a series of significant barriers, from the busy noise of coaches to the frightening bustle of airports to the confusing complexity of driving a car. The issues that I will explore in this section are all pretty serious – after all, the ability to move around and get to places is very important, and the autistic community as a whole has real difficulty in managing to maintain this kind of freedom.

Believe it or not, and Google's predictive searches would suggest that this is a surprise to many, autistic people *can* learn to drive and become very good drivers. I learned to drive later than most, in my mid-twenties. This was partly a result of my aforementioned inability to plan in advance, as sorting out driving lessons and tests requires a level of personal organisation that's usually well beyond my reach. It was also because as a child I'd not experienced having a car as an inalienable fact of life. Unlike all my friends and relatives, my family didn't have one for the majority of my childhood. This was mostly a financial decision as we weren't very well off, but it was also down to my father's lack of interest in driving as an activity. As a consequence, the idea of owning and driving around in a car was as distant and abstract as, well, the idea of having a book published and available in the shops. It was only when an ex-partner of mine was learning herself that I began to get used to the idea and, with a considerable amount of help from her, I managed to navigate the stressful world of learner drivers and get myself the valuable licence that would allow me to scoot around the country at my leisure.

And I do enjoy it. Driving uses up just enough of my brain that I experience unusual quietude when on the road, and most of my best and calmest thinking is done when driving on the motorway. Given that such relaxation and mental stillness are very rare for me, this's a huge bonus. Unfortunately, it's a very expensive way to encourage peaceful thought, so I cannot utilise it as much as I'd like, for both my wallet's and the planet's sake. Having said all of that, though, driving is still challenging in its own way, mostly thanks to the unpredictability of the other people on the road.

Communicative differences in other parts of life transfer into the world of driving, after all, meaning that the methods of communication used by drivers can cause me enormous stress and worry. Take, for example, the time-honoured (in the UK at least) brief flash of the full beams. Now, I know from experience that this is used mostly to deliver thanks, perhaps for giving way down a narrow street. But I'm also aware that it can be used to signal irritation and anger, ironically most often, perhaps, when I've accidentally left my lights on full beam while driving towards an oncoming vehicle, like Christine in the Stephen King novel. As a result, there's considerable confusion about the gesture, to the point that I never end up using it myself, as I'm terrified of people getting the wrong end of the stick from my frantic flashing of head-lights.

Similarly, I've an extremely dysfunctional relationship with car horns. Other people seem to use them all the time, for all sorts of reasons, and weirdly always seem perfectly poised to let out a firm 'honk' whenever the need arises. I'm absolutely bewildered by this, because on the few occasions when I've been put in severe danger by another driver, the last thing I thought to do was announce my displeasure by finding exactly the right part of the steering wheel to pummel with my fist. Instead I tend to be more absorbed in using the steering wheel, clutch and brakes to bring myself to a safe, if sweaty and unhappy, stop. I cannot see why I'd have made these situations more complicated for me by adding an angry parp into the mix. I view the car horn in the same way as I view my own full shouting voice: a potent tool that really doesn't need to be used except in exceptional circumstances. It's likely that this is based, in part, on my own autistic response to hearing car horns blare – I'm no fan of sudden loud noises.

If the communicative options when driving my own vehicle are difficult enough, using public transport involves a whole new level of trickiness. I've lived in cities with reasonably good bus services in the past – both Nottingham and Bristol boast ones that actually exist and generally manage to take you where you wish to go – and I've consequently been a bus user many, many times. However, I can't say that I enjoy the experience. Taking the bus is a real challenge for this particular autistic person.

Bus travel, however, is very important to the autistic population. We don't earn as much, on average, as the neurotypical community and many of us are in pretty desperate financial straits (if you wish to know why this may be, I encourage you to re-read the first six chapters of this book …). As a result, taking the bus may be the only means we have to get to places that are some distance away. Couple this with the fact that autism is fairly regularly paired up with a physical disability that may make walking difficult, with Ehlers–Danlos syndrome being a particularly common 'partner', and you can see why autistic people rely on buses quite a lot. Which is a shame, because the experience of travelling by bus is so extraordinarily draining and awful for autistic people in general.

First there's the unpredictability. In an amusing joke played on us by city councils and bus companies, bus timetables are dotted around at every bus stop, confidently proclaiming that the next bus to Bristol Temple Meads will be at 9.47 a.m. Such precision suggests unerring accuracy, and like a fool I've always taken these at face value and arrived, fresh-faced and innocent, at the stop ahead of time, looking forward to a simple and stress-free journey. Reality strikes with the realisation that bus timetables are a simple fiction. For someone who needs things to work as advertised so that my routine can be maintained as best as possible, the fact that the 9.47 a.m. bus could arrive at any time between 9.30 a.m. and 10.30 a.m. is not very helpful. The advent of live updates on those dot-matrix displays in the more sophisticated bus stops has been a big help, but only insofar as they confirm what you suspected anyway: your bus will not arrive when you expected it to.

My logical brain understands why this is, of course. Unlike train lines, which are closely monitored and used by far fewer vehicles, bus times are dependent on human traffic – all those people driving cars and honking randomly at one another – and, as a result, maintaining set times is pretty difficult. But this doesn't change the fact that it makes the bus system pretty unusable for autistic people at times.

Then there's the fact that bus services are almost always packed to the brim with humanity. In my childhood I'd often board a rattling, tiny 'Fox Cub' bus (back in the 1990s all the bus companies in Leicestershire celebrated the county's predilection for chasing and murdering foxes while on horseback) to go and see my grandparents. These buses were always completely empty, and they clanked their way merrily through the English countryside without a care. I loved these journeys. In adulthood I realised what an aberration they were and that, in the cities at least, buses would be filled right up to their capacity. On a sensory basis, this is very difficult for autistic people to manage. The noise and smell and heat get stifling and extremely uncomfortable, and the feeling of a stranger pressed right up against my shoulder and legs becomes overwhelming. I cannot count the number of times I'd dismount a bus in Bristol in the same manner as a person escaping a huge mosh-pit at a Slipknot gig, gasping for air and bruised by the endless jostling. These days, if I've got to take a bus (thankfully rare because I simply don't go anywhere), I have to factor in the fact that it's guaranteed to push me close to meltdown, and plan the rest of my day accordingly.

Trains are better. There's something far more regimented and organised about a train journey. Yes, we can laugh at how unreliable they are in the UK, but they're still an awful lot better than the bus network. Trains are regular, they follow easy-to-understand routes through the country and wait an awful lot longer at their stops than buses do (for anyone with a physical disability, the milliseconds that buses spend waiting is extremely unhelpful). I've had the opportunity plenty of times to re-board a train in order to recover a piece of luggage I've left behind and still get back off again before the train trundled off. For somebody with severe executive dysfunction, this is brilliant.

They tend to be a bit more spacious too, and usually have air conditioning that actually works, helping to filter out the worst of the heat and smells that can cause serious issues on buses. They have helpful members of staff that can be called upon in an emergency, and stations often have lots of amenities. Having said all that, for some autistic people train travel can still be taxing. Timetables are ridiculously difficult to navigate – those huge walls of numbers that you see at stations are totally inaccessible, unless you really know what you're doing. Station buildings – especially the big ones (I'm looking at you, Birmingham) – can be labyrinthine and unhelpful, with hidden platforms and toilets accessible only to those who somehow still carry spare change in the 2020s. Stations are also often noisy and dirty, with the peace broken every ten seconds or so by that descending chirrup of ding-dongs that notifies us that an unintelligible announcement is about to be made. For autistic people who can struggle to filter sounds, trying to decipher what the announcer is saying against a backdrop of diesel engines revving, children shouting and whistles blowing can be impossible.

But nothing – absolutely nothing – comes close to the nightmare of the airport.

Everything about air travel seems to have been purpose-built to destroy autistic people. I doubt this was the intention, of course, but that's how it appears. Rather similar to schools, really. And workplaces. And the world. The big issue with air travel is the sensory bombardment throughout the entire experience. Airports are huge and either egregiously crowded or eerily empty – there doesn't appear to be any scale in between – so we're either jostled and hassled by thousands of people all pulling vast wheeled suitcases, and cowed by the awful noise and constant announcements, or sitting in an empty, echoing hall completely alone, terrified that we've misread the date and time of the flight and thinking that maybe the terminal has been earmarked for explosive demolition this morning. Neither are fun.

The system that exists to convey passengers onto flights is a real challenge. Hours are spent (we take very seriously the advice to arrive fourteen hours before the flight is scheduled) staring at the departure boards and waiting for our gate to be called, only to realise that the numbering of the gates in the terminal seems to be based purely on chaos rather than logic. When we eventually find the correct endless corridor to walk down, the fear that we've messed up somehow becomes unbearable. After all, the stakes are high and the system is so horribly confusing – there's a real fear that the plane will fly off and leave us behind, lost in a maze of moving floors and perfume shops.

Eventually the gate itself becomes visible and anxiety drops a little, until we realise just how busy it is. Watching people arrive and fill the many seats becomes rather like watching floodwaters rise in your living room; all we can manage is quiet resignation and a feeling that things are going to get much worse before they get better. Those faint hopes that I might perhaps get a seat to myself with no one next to me evaporate. A total lack of official representation causes anxiety to renew – Where are the airline people who will let us onto the plane? Have I got the right gate? What's going on? – and by the time I'm ensconced safely in my seat (realising too late that I've left my noise-cancelling headphones in the overhead bins), I'm already a nervous wreck. I haven't been on a plane for six years and, frankly, I'm perfectly happy with that.

One of my special interests has always been air disasters. I don't know why, but they fascinate and horrify me in equal measure. I must have read up on hundreds of accidents over the course of my life. It may be a result of having seen the Kegworth air disaster on the M1 motorway from my bedroom window as a kid – events like that tend to have long repercussions – but, whatever the cause, I know every single one of the myriad things that might bring a plane down from the air. So, as you can imagine, the period of time where my flight is, indeed, airborne is rather tense and unhappy, with every beep, creak and judder noticed by my over-sensitive ears and eyes, and analysed against my huge databanks of awful catastrophe. Not every autistic flyer will have this particular difficulty, but it's a nice illustration of how special interests can really come back and bite you on the arse.

There are a few things that could be done to improve all forms of travel for autistic people:

- Include us in the group of disabled people who get first access to the aircraft cabin. Being given the opportunity to climb aboard and settle ourselves down before the rolling tide of humanity embarks would be a great help to our stress levels, I believe. I would like to think that this is already standard, but given how autism is so frequently not included as a disability in situations like this, I'm sceptical.

- Ensure that airports are more clearly signposted. Lots of effort is put into making them multilingual, for obvious reasons – perhaps a little effort could go into making the process of moving through the airport more transparent and less dependent on whether you've done it before. To be honest, this would be a boon for autistic people who like things to make logical, clear sense, but also to pretty much every other human being that wanders confused through the halls.

- When it comes to train and bus travel we once again have the issue of education – of ensuring that drivers, conductors and ticket salespeople are well versed in neurodiversity as a concept and understand how being autistic might affect their passengers' experience. A little compassion when everything is going wrong can go a long way.

- Finally, if you're in a position to lessen an autistic person's need to travel, then do it. Rather than meeting us halfway, maybe you can meet at ours (or at least closer to us); perhaps you can do the driving for us, or meet us at the station and travel with us? There may be a multitude of ways to reduce the stress associated with travel.

And what's the best thing about travel? When you arrive, you have to do all of it again, only in reverse, and possibly in a place where no one speaks your language.

8

THE NEED FOR JUSTICE

RIGHT AND WRONG

There's an enduring myth that all autistic people are faultlessly logical, that our brains are computer-like in their strict application of rules and facts, that our way of viewing the world is not far removed from the way you might imagine a spreadsheet would view it. As with so many of society's most firmly held ideas about autism, this is a fallacy – the real story is much more complicated than this. There is, however, a grain of truth in there: for a huge number of autistic people there's a greater expectation of consistency, of the world abiding by its own rules.

Autistic people often seem to have a very deep and strong sense of what's right, what's reasonable and what's fair. This is not to say that we're unerring moral arbiters; after all, our sense of what's fair may be affected by any number of factors, such as privilege, experience, upbringing and so on, and therefore not match others' opinions and values. Nevertheless, the *strength* of feeling and conviction is likely to be a feature for many autistic people.

I saw this an awful lot at school while I was teaching. Autistic students could never let an injustice drop. If another child was told off by the teacher for something – I don't know, perhaps throwing a paper aeroplane or plugging wall sockets with Play-Doh – and the autistic student knew that this kid wasn't responsible, it was highly likely that they'd demand to see justice done. I've seen students who'd never speak up, never rock the boat in any direction, become incandescent with righteous anger at a teacher doling out unfair punishment. This expectation of propriety seems to be a common part of autistic experience.

Central to this is an expectation that the world will consistently make sense, that cause and effect will be doggedly adhered to, and that truth and reason will always win out against lies and fantasy.

I don't think many of us handle very well the realisation that the world simply doesn't work that way.

UNREASONABLE WORLD

I hope it's clear to you by now that the world as it currently exists is not well set up for autistic people, and that this is a constant source of misery. All of the sensory pressure, the difficulty with planning, the endless problems communicating with our fellow human beings – it all contributes to the feeling that the world is hostile and unpleasant. Sadly, however, that's only the beginning, for it's the irrationalities of the world, the peculiar behaviours, attitudes, hatreds and prejudices that can really make us feel unwelcome visitors to a strange world.

In my experience, autistic people are good pattern spotters and often excellent at working out the rules of any given situation. This is what makes us so good at masking, after all. We figure out the rules, and then we play the game. The problem is that figuring out the rules doesn't prepare you for how to handle those who decide to cheat. In the game of Planet Earth, the rules are easy to understand and, arguably, pretty easy to abide by. Don't lie, don't hurt other people, don't treat people badly, be kind, fair and honest. I've never needed religion to understand this – it's as self-evident as the water cycle or the wind in the trees. And yet so many people don't seem to find it necessary to follow these rules at all.

For example, people lie as if it's going out of fashion especially these days. Small lies are bad enough, the kind that your friends may tell when exaggerating their achievements or when my daughter refuses to own up to the exact reason why there's glitter over every square inch of the living-room carpet. These lies corrode in their own way, and it can be difficult to see the point of such trivial little untruths. But it's the bigger lies, told by bigger people and organisations, that really stretch my understanding. They're often so far removed from reality, so easily disproven, that I struggle to understand what the benefit is for the liar – at least in the long term. As far as I can see, the world can only operate properly if truth is adhered to. If we want society, the world and human civilisation to continue to thrive and develop, then the truth must be maintained at all costs. This is as basic as it gets, and yet still everybody lies.

Politicians lie about their actions, their aims, ambitions and policies. Corporations lie about their profits, their impact on the ecosphere, their treatment of employees. Nations lie about their foreign policy, their wars and the well-being of their populations. Everywhere I look in the twenty-first century there are lies built upon lies, to the point that it's almost impossible to fathom what on earth the truth is anymore.

I suppose that's the point.

This is disorientating for everyone, but I believe autistic people suffer even harder in such an environment. It may be because we're less persuaded by bullshit, or perhaps because we recognise lies as being naturally dangerous; whatever, autistic people *feel* the effects of this destruction of order and reason very strongly. We're so wedded to routine, patterns and predictability, in order to survive our soaring stress levels, that whenever the world at large 'goes rogue' and seems to defy basic logic – and examples could include, but are not limited to, the terrifying inaction on climate change and the inability of the world's population to consistently handle the impact of Covid-19 – we're left completely confused and unable to accept what's happening.

It has always seemed to me that a large portion of the population can accept this nonsense with a shrug of the shoulders. 'Ah, politicians always lie,' they say, ignoring the fact that the lies have been growing in size and impact by orders of magnitude for decades. 'Ah, it'll be

OK – I like warm weather,' they announce when told of the disastrous climate outcomes we're so studiously ignoring. But I can't do this, and nor can many of my autistic kin. We're unable to ignore these bad signs. We can't shrug our shoulders and get on with things. Instead, we argue, we fight, we protest, we kick up a fuss. We're not unique in this, of course; lots of non-autistic people are fighting the good fight here too, but I feel that autistic people can be particularly focused and single-minded on these issues. This is, when you think about it, quite useful at the moment.

One of the most famous people on Earth right now is autistic. Greta Thunberg has never wavered in her basic communication of simple scientific facts about the oncoming climate disaster. Her initial protest, of refusing to go to school while at the same time raising awareness of the problem, is as simple as it has been effective. Not allowing herself to get mired in the nonsensical counter-arguments offered by those in thrall to the fossil fuel industries, Thunberg has consistently delivered the same message: listen to the scientists if you want the world to continue to exist. The simplicity of this message is, in my opinion, a touchstone of autistic clarity. There's no effort to sugar the pill, no attempt to meet the bad-faith opposition halfway, because there's no point in doing so. If society is to survive, and humanity is to thrive, we must listen to the science and make improvements to how we treat the planet.

It's this clarity of thought, impervious to irrelevant distraction, that I believe is something of an autistic trait. I try my hardest to avoid the 'autism as superpower' trope, as it's very damaging given how difficult life is for autistic people, but in this instance it comes close to the truth. Some people have even argued that this is what autism is *for*, which is a fascinating if misguided idea. I don't believe autism is 'for' anything; it simply *is*, and we can choose to either make the best of what it offers the world or not. It is, however, certainly very interesting to wonder whether autistic people might carve a niche for themselves, where this ability to cut through the bull and get to the core of the issue becomes an agent of powerful change in our highly polarised, confusing and precarious world. I hate disability 'inspiration porn', but I do sometimes wonder whether autistic people might just save the world ...

Being autistic does not automatically grant you these 'powers', though. When I say that clarity of thought seems to be an autistic trait, the heavy lifting is done by the word 'seems', and I wouldn't want to give the impression that autistic people are beyond reproach, and always behave in a perfectly moral and good way. We don't.

Autistic people can be vulnerable, for example, to peer pressure, which can lead to very bad outcomes. I believe that autistic boys and young men are, for example, particularly vulnerable to far-right ideologies, given that such ideas are disarmingly simple and based on clear logic (us vs them, scapegoating and so on). Without the knowledge needed to appreciate how hollow and vicious these ideologies really are, they can be very enticing. With careful manipulation by others, autistic young people might find themselves immersed in dangerous discourse, especially online, and gradually find themselves supporting views and ideas that are beyond the pale. After years of being ostracised and treated poorly by their peers in real life, it may even be understandable why they might fall for the tempting lies offered by such political beliefs.

And if that isn't a good enough reason to ensure that all autistic children are supported and more carefully nurtured through the hostilities of their schooldays, then I really don't know what is.

Autistic people often seem to understand the fundamental issues very well and are unperturbed by flailing distractions to try to throw us off the scent. In a natural continuation of monotropism, we may well be better than average at keeping our eyes on what really matters and can use that to our advantage to create change, so long as we're healthy enough to do so. There are a huge number of things that stand in our way, though.

FIGHTING AGAINST PREJUDICE

When disabled people suffer at the hands of prejudice and a lack of accommodation, it's called 'ableism'. Like all of the other related '-isms', this is the result of a combination of ignorance and wilful mistreatment of a minority by whoever the majority may consist of. It's interesting to note that ableism is yet to experience the kind of large-scale awareness-raising and fightback that – thank heavens – racism, homophobia and sexism have all experienced to a greater or lesser degree (the results of which are still far from enough). Ableism has continued to spread and be perpetuated fairly freely, and, despite recent waves of improved awareness and a shifting in values, still appears to be at an endemic stage where it has a large and mostly unacknowledged impact on the lives of disabled people.

Autistic people are disabled – either because society is inaccessible and unsuited to us, or because autism is inherently disabling whatever the societal structure (this is something many autistic people disagree about) – and as such we can be victims of ableism. Indeed, many of the difficulties and unreasonable treatments I've outlined earlier in this book would count as examples of ableism, from the inability of the NHS to adapt itself to the autistic neurotype to the way that workplaces insist on following unwritten rules. It all constitutes a lack of awareness, acceptance and accommodation for autistic people that's very harmful to us. However, my relationship with disability as a concept, and therefore ableism as a threat, is complex.

The problem for me is that I was diagnosed with autism so late in life. Other than being autistic, ADHD and having severe depression, I have no other disabilities, and these three only became apparent to me in my mid-to-late thirties. As such, I lived the majority of my life completely unaware that I *was* actually disabled, and – to be brutally honest – gave disabled concerns relatively little thought. Imposter syndrome is common with late-diagnosed autistic people, and it works overtime with me. Although I now know and accept that I'm disabled, I still feel a phony, a faker, a charlatan. This isn't rational (what in imposter's syndrome is?) but it is *potent*, making me feel like I'm over-reacting when responding to ableism, as if it shouldn't upset me because I'm not *really* autistic.

I mention this here mostly in solidarity with fellow autistic people who may feel the same way. Autism is known as an invisible disability, and it can be hard to appreciate that our challenges and struggles are worthy of being classed as a disability. But I must place that to one side and explore some distinct examples of ableism that autistic people will confront, beyond the many hundreds of accessibility issues I've spoken of so far in the preceding chapters.

First, let's consider language use. The words we employ to describe ourselves may seem a trivial thing, and to a certain extent the example I will share is relatively benign compared with the language issues that can exist for some other minority groups, but it's indicative of a wider problem, a broader malaise that needs to be countered wherever possible. You may have noticed that throughout this book I've referred to my neurotype kin as 'autistic people' rather than 'people with autism'. This is a *very* conscious choice. The problem with 'people with autism' is that it makes autism sound like a piece of baggage that we carry around – an albatross around our neck, dragging us down. Lots of us don't feel this is accurate representation. Instead, 'autistic people' brings our autistic-ness to the fore, highlights it as a key part of our existence, and makes it clear it's not something we're ashamed of.

But it's more than that. It's also a very handy way of determining whether someone is listening. Autistic people are used to people not listening: ignoring us as we talk about our interests, ignoring us as we explain ourselves, ignoring us as we expend energy trying to get everyone to understand that they share the planet with different neurotypes. And watching non-autistic people butt in on conversations online with an over-confident, 'Oh, you shouldn't say autistic person – it's *person with autism*' is an immediate sign that this particular individual is clearly not listening to the fact that the vast majority of autistic people (over 80 per cent of respondents at the last count, I believe) reject person-first language. This happens, I regret to say, an awful lot. We've taken to calling it 'ablesplaining', for obvious reasons.

One of the reasons it hurts so much that our voices are unheard is because we're not getting any assistance from the rest of the world. In our push, this last ten years or so, to be more widely understood, accepted and even appreciated, we've had to consistently push against the endless churn of poor-quality representation in the media.

This is a vital thing. Seeing your own group represented accurately and positively in media productions, from film to television, can have an enormous impact on both the minority community and the community at large. As an example, I'm overjoyed at how LEGO are continuing to widen their representation of everyone in their minifigures (the little people that populate their sets). This year, for example, we've seen the first LEGO minifigure with a prosthetic leg, while there have been wheelchair users in LEGO sets for a few years now. These are good, positive representation of disabilities, and they can go a long way towards boosting confidence and raising awareness.

When we look for autistic representation in the media, though, all we find are poor-quality stereotypes of varied degrees of unpleasantness. Apart from a few notable exceptions, like the great little show *Everything's Gonna Be Okay*, and books by writers such as Elle McNicoll and Holly Smale (both of whose characters benefit massively from the fact the authors themselves are neurodivergent), we're presented with autistic characters who do very little to challenge the old, unacceptable caricatures that date back to *Rain Man* and beyond.

In the last few years the *cause célèbre* has been the musician Sia's film *Music*, where we have a non-autistic person playing an autistic role in a way that's genuinely offensive to huge numbers of autistic people the world over. Seeing non-autistic people playing autistic roles, and non-autistic people writing scripts about autistic people, is jarring and, if we stop to clear our heads and think for a moment, completely unacceptable. There are many autistic writers and actors out there trying to break into the world of media, and yet their places are almost always snatched up by people who have an autistic nephew and believe this is enough to enable them to start making films about autism. The autistic community would benefit massively from seeing itself accurately represented on screen. It would give a group of people who often lack confidence and feel like we're not part of any kind of 'in crowd' a huge boost, and at the same time would educate the general population on what the autistic experience really is. But sadly, it feels like we're still a long way off this.

And, would you believe it, it doesn't stop there. An ongoing problem that causes considerable consternation both in the UK and the USA is the fact that charities and organisations ostensibly set up to help autistic people (or at least their parents …) often have no one who is autistic anywhere in their leadership structure. Our lack of representation in the media is an avoidable problem; lack of autistic representation in the charities that exist to support us is an absolute disaster. After all, there's absolutely no excuse. Although I admit I'd be terrible at the job, there are hundreds if not thousands of autistic people who'd be able to bring amazing insight into these charities, as well as run them soundly at the same time. There are a few positive stories in this regard – the CEO of the Irish national autistic charity (AsIAm Ireland) is autistic, and some British charities are at least *trying* to improve things, but I can't think of a more potent symbol of how overlooked and ignored autistic people are than this.

And it pisses me off. Because of course it does; I'm autistic, and it's just not reasonable.

ADVOCACY IN A TYPICAL WORLD

I've been an 'advocate' for autism in online spaces for about five years now. I fell into it almost by accident (like almost every other aspect of my life, as you may have noticed), after I wrote long Twitter threads on my own experience of being autistic. These proved to be very popular, and as a result here I am: writing a book about everything I've learned about being autistic since I was diagnosed. But my knowledge and experience have natural limitations, and I want to finish this book by acknowledging this and by signposting where you should go next in your exploration of what it is to be autistic.

Autism is the great leveller – every conceivable demographic on the planet has an autistic population, but these communities are not fairly represented by the vast majority of high-profile autistic advocates. Like almost any other space, the autistic community is dominated by the voices of white, speaking, cis and Western people, often (though not exclusively) fairly middle class. Obviously, I fit into this demographic myself, and as a result I must recommend one thing: use this book as a *starting point*.

If autistic people the world over are going to get the fair and reasonable treatment that we deserve, then it's imperative that every flavour of autistic experience has a chance of being heard and understood. In order for this to happen, people need to be made aware of the voices and writing of the more marginalised communities that exist within the autism population as a whole, because the impact of these intersections on how autism manifests and affects lives is huge.

One of the key demographics within the autistic community that I wish to raise awareness of is the non-speaking community. For years we've used the term 'non-verbal' for autistics who do not use the spoken word to communicate, but it's clear how completely unhelpful and inaccurate this term is. 'Non-verbal' suggests a lack of any kind of language use – a complete inability to put feelings and thoughts into words that can be communicated, but this is far from the truth for many non-speaking autistic people. Non-speaking autistic people, for the most part, are fully verbal internally, with the same rich inner thoughts and ideas as anyone else, but of course are not as able to communicate these thoughts and ideas with the outside world. As a result, inaccurate assumptions are made about their capabilities and their lives, assumptions that become hard to shake, and that eventually morph into stereotypes and prejudices.

It's when you enter the world of non-speaking autistic advocacy that you realise just how wrong all of these assumptions are. From the startling insight on the pages of *The Reason I Jump* by Naoki Higashida to the brilliant blogs of non-speakers such as Hari Srinivasan and the speeches of Elizabeth Bonker, we can now access a wealth of information about what it is to be non-speaking, autistic and inhabiting the world. Using a variety of methods to enable their words to be recorded, including technology such as AAC (alternative and augmented communication), non-speakers have much to add to autistic discourse and to advocacy in generally, but their words are not as widely shared as those of speaking autistic people, and so tend to be overlooked by non-autistics attempting to understand our world. Thankfully, the written medium of the internet allows all autistic people, speaking or not, to reach an audience, so long as the audience knows that they're there.

It's worth noting at this point that being non-speaking is something of a continuum of its own. Some autistic people are completely non-speaking, and will use technological or person-led assistance to communicate in all situations. Other autistic people are non-speaking only sometimes, often depending on the scenario or the person's stress levels. Almost all autistic people may experience what it is to be non-speaking for short periods, perhaps, for example, during a shut-down. I find that when my stress levels reach a particular point, my voice begins to falter as a tool, becoming less reliable and less focused, and I begin to lose my vocabulary and grammar. The spoken word is by no means guaranteed in the autistic community, and we don't deserve to be overlooked as a result of this.

This includes those autistic people who also have learning disabilities, who may be less able to communicate their experiences and needs with the world, and rely on proxies (such as parents or carers) to argue their corner. There has to be concerted effort from the non-autistic world to hear all of these viewpoints, and autistic people who do have a voice must remind them of this fact.

* * *

There are stories that it's not my place to tell within other intersections of autism. The Black autistic community, especially in the USA, works hard to raise awareness and understanding of the particular difficulties that Black autistics face. One challenge that has always stood out for me is the heightened value of masking – how Black autistics cannot unmask as freely as white autistic people may be able to (when circumstances permit) because of the added threat of racist interpretation of behaviour. If the stimming of a white person can be interpreted very badly by the neurotypical population, the stimming of a Black autistic person could be misinterpreted even more unpleasantly, with results a thousand times worse.

I remember being educated on this very topic one time – rightly so – when I entreated autistic people to take the opportunity to unmask whenever possible, for our own health. A number of Twitter accounts reminded me of the danger of this for many Black autistics, and my eyes were opened to the huge number of areas where advocacy must adapt and see the differences in situations. But as I say, these are not my stories to tell: get online, find the communities and begin to listen.

There's a huge crossover between the autistic and trans communities. It's too early to say why this is, as research is in its infancy. However, I'm inclined to agree with the idea that it's a result of autistic people feeling less bound by the established rules of society and more likely to go with what fits them, and damn the expectations of the neuro-majority. This would certainly lead to a greater number of autistic people accepting that they're trans and moving forward, rather than perhaps denying the issue. However, with trans rights under heavy attack, especially in the UK at the time of writing, we see the overlap between the autistic and trans communities being weaponised by those who seek to discredit trans concerns and rights. Too often I read about how 'vulnerable' autistic people are 'targeted' by the trans community, and are therefore forced into being trans against their will.

Autistic people may be many things, but being vulnerable to such nefarious schemes (if such schemes even exist, which I'm certain they don't) is not one of them. Too many of us have spent hour after hour analysing our own behaviour, going over things in minute detail so as to be completely *sure*, to determine that we are, in fact, autistic – a conclusion that seems to almost always be borne out by official diagnosis. It stands to reason, therefore, that we possess the faculty to make similar decisions about our gender and sexuality.

A WORLD BUILT FOR US

The intersections of autism all deserve to be heard equally so that every autistic person, no matter their demographic, can live their best life in a world that's built for them. Because that's ultimately what all of this *has* to be about – the world is a hostile, terrifying place for autistic people everywhere, for so many reasons, that even in a middling-size book like this I've only scratched the surface. For as long as this continues, autistic people of all backgrounds and life experiences are going to suffer. They will suffer reduced life expectancy, reduced lifetime income, reduced opportunities, reduced likelihood of starting a family, reduced ability to live a life that's true to them, reduced safety on the streets, reduced provision at school, at work, on public transport, in every town, city and country in the world. This cannot be allowed to continue.

If we're to see real equity between the neurotypical majority and the autistic minority, then things have to change. The status quo is no good. It leads to meltdown, burnout and early death for a significant portion of the population. Remember that as many as one in twenty people may be autistic and that it's possible that one in five are neurodivergent in some way. This is a lot of people to condemn to misery by stubbornly refusing to change tack. In the United Kingdom alone we're probably talking about at least three million individuals, all with hopes, dreams, lives and relationships, and all struggling under the weight of living in a hostile world that could so easily be transformed into a friendly one.

Ensure that everybody has a better understanding of what autism is, so that autism as a neurotype is as well understood and casually discussed as the difference between introverts and extroverts. A world where everyone knows the true basics of autism and rejects the old stereotypes is within reach. Autistic people such as myself are eager to share this information with you, in the hope that it may improve things not just for us, but for our children and grandchildren. Get this information in the media, normalise autistic characters is books, films, TV shows and soap operas, and have them played or written by actual autistic people. Open up the taboo of disability in schools and workplaces, and make autism as a difference be something that's celebrated and talked about openly.

Imagine a world where people can say, 'Oh, do you mind if we don't shake hands? I'm autistic, you see,' and be acknowledged and treated as an equal. Where autistic children can feel safe in schools that completely understand their needs and don't treat them as oddities. Where autistic older people can retire in comfort, knowing that they'll be properly supported should they need twenty-four-hour care, by people who understand autism and recognise their behaviour as normal, rather than weird or alarming.

It feels so easy, because it is. The information is there, we just need people to read it and listen to it. The 1 to 10 per cent of us that share the planet with you need you to make this effort – at last, after all these years – to accept us into your world, to take this neurotypical world and make it untypical; an untypical world that's genuinely built for everybody.

APPENDIX

There are many excellent resources for anyone who, after reading this book, is keen to dive in and find out more about the overall autistic experience. The first and most immediate source of this information is social media, where you'll find thousands upon thousands of autistic people all trying to share their existence with the world. With a careful use of hashtags and search terms you'll be able to find autistic communities in every demographic.

Beyond Twitter, Facebook and Instagram (and also TikTok, but I cannot pretend to know how that actually works), there are a large number of organisations that you can look into for further information from actual autistic people. One that I can recommend for its sheer volume of excellent content is Neuroclastic.com – an autistic-run news/aggregate site that collects together some of the best writing from autistic people across the world. Another excellent starting point is the American site Autastic.com, which is a good gateway into autistic

Black, Indigenous and people of colour (BIPOC) issues and experience.

Beyond the web, there are many books published every year by autistic writers, and that's the key to look for: always focus on books about autism written by people who are themselves autistic. For years, autistic people's only representation in literature (both fiction and non-fiction) were those neurotypical people who deigned to write about us. Now there are hundreds of autistic authors writing about just about every aspect of autism, so dive in and continue to deepen your understanding.

ACKNOWLEDGEMENTS

I'd like to take a moment to thank everyone who has helped me complete this book. First, my editor at HarperCollins, Anna Mrowiec, for taking a chance with a just-starting-out writer struggling to get by. Also to my agent James Spackman for his invaluable advice and support when writing and pitching the book in the first place. I'd also like to thank my friends for their advice and confidence in my work, especially Nial Busby for being so relentlessly nice and showering me with pictures of his trainset layout, and to Sara Gibbs for helping me get through the day-to-day tribulations and anxieties associated with writing books.

Thanks also to my friends in the autistic community on Twitter for being so supportive of my writing from day one, and putting up with my constant moaning. Particular thanks go to those individuals who provided excellent little details and anecdotes for my chapters: Fergus Murray for his instructive expertise on the concept of monotropism, Hazel (@AnLasair) for their take on phone calls, Teresa B (@Trees_in_Winter) for their feelings on school group work, Charlie (@ Charlie28352975) for their experience of getting doctor appointments and Samuel Ramsden (@gwyrdhanmor) for sharing his love of watch straps.

On top of these specific shout-outs, I have to thank the following for their always insightful and hugely valuable advocacy on neurodivergent topics: Ann Memmott, Kieran Rose, Dr Amy Pearson, Luke Beardon, Dr Georgia Pavlopoulou, Emily Burke, Lauren Ellzey, Emma Dalmayne, Païvi Butcher, Liam O'Dell, Dr Damien Milton, Sara Gibbs (again), Joanne Limburg, Holly Smale, Riah Person, Ella Tabb, Pastiche Graham, Eric Garcia, Robert Chapman, Monique Botha and Steve Silberman. There are so many more.

Finally, I'd like to thank my partner for putting up with so much of my nonsense, and my parents and my sister for being there, being them and, well, everything.